Instructor's Manual for

MANAGING CLASSROOM BEHAVIOR
A Reflective Case-Based Approach

Prepared by

James M. Kauffman
University of Virginia

Mark P. Mostert
Moorhead State University

Deborah G. Nuttycombe
University of Northern Iowa

Stanley C. Trent
Michigan State University

Daniel P. Hallahan
University of Virginia

ALLYN AND BACON
BOSTON LONDON TORONTO SYDNEY TOKYO SINGAPORE

ISBN 0-205-14696-1

Printed in the United States of America

10 9 8 7 6 5 4 3 2 1   97 96 95 94 93 92

Table of Contents

WHAT YOU DON'T KNOW CAN HURT YOU! John McCullum
Precis. A student teacher in general education runs into problems with a class of diverse eighth graders when he tries to manage a group activity in his supervising teacher's absence, ending up in a protracted power struggle with one male student who, he later learns, has been in a class for students with emotional or behavioral disorders.

GRANDMA'S BOY: Helen Jamison
Precis. Part A: Early in her first year of teaching second grade, a teacher encounters difficulty in working with the father and grandmother of a boy who is having serious academic and behavioral problems.
Part B: With consultation from a school psychologist, the teacher attempts to use behavior contracts, but these are unsuccessful and result in the student's emotional outburst, leaving her feeling defeated.

IS KEVIN BLUFFING? Carol Yake
Precis. An experienced sixth grade teacher must deal with a crisis when one of her students, a boy diagnosed as psychotic but spending most of the school day in her regular classroom, appears ready to jump from a second story staircase.

THEY FAILED DERRICK: Melinda Smith

Precis. Part A: An experienced teacher of children with mental retardation, now teaching a regular fifth grade class, volunteers to take a student with a distinguished history of violent and threatening behavior, and now she must confront him about bringing a knife to school.

Part B: Although the teacher handles him masterfully, the student frightens the assistant principal and is placed first in a special class in a middle school and, later, in a mental hospital, leading the teacher to conclude that everyone has failed him.

THE FAIRY GODMOTHERS: Paul Miller

Precis. Part A: An experienced English teacher with a recent graduate degree in special education takes a mid-year position teaching 11-, 12-, and 13-year-olds with learning disabilities, discovers that the previous teacher apparently offered little or no effective instruction or behavior management and left her position precipitously, and finds that his aide and a young substitute apparently have only entertained the students with games for the previous three weeks.

Part B: Having taken over the class from the substitute, the teacher must deal with his students' use of racial epithets, their organized plan to test his instructional skills and authority, and a direct challenge from the group's ringleader.

THE PHANTOM PREGNANCY: Barbara Thompson

Precis. A regular classroom teacher struggles with how to respond to a 12-year-old girl in her class who, in addition to having learning disabilities and emotional or behavioral disorders, believes that she is pregnant from sexual abuse by her mother's boyfriend and insists that she wants to be sexually active and become pregnant.

STEALING TIME: Robert Carter

Precis. Part A: An experienced fourth-grade teacher who has a highly structured classroom that produces good results with many students with disabilities has increasing difficulty with a boy who has learning disabilities and problems with his peers, culminating in suspicion that he has stolen a classmate's watch.

Part B: The teacher determines that the boy has stolen the watch and must decide how to handle his continuing suspicion, and that of classmates, that the boy is stealing other items.

THE TRUTH ABOUT ALICE: Janet Lane

Precis. An experienced algebra teacher discovers belatedly that a rumor about an unattractive girl is contributing to her low social status, and in the context of apparent teasing by a group of boys the teacher wonders how she can help this student understand what is happening to her without eroding her self-image and social status even further.

ONE BAD APPLE: Elaine Brown

Precis. A veteran teacher, now teaching the group of fifth graders that she had in fourth grade, is confronted with problems created by two new boys, one of whom exhibits aggressive antisocial behavior, and soon finds herself enmeshed in coercive relationships with them as a means of maintaining her control.

THE CONTRACT WITH PARRISH AND SON: Rebecca Phillips
Precis. A middle school special education teacher finds that her typical behavior management system is insufficient for a new student, but her attempts to involvehis father result in the student's apparent physical abuse, indications of depression, and a crisis in which he curses her and runs out of the room.

THE MASCOT: Cathy Anderson
Precis. A student teacher in a resource class for 11- to 13-year-olds with learning disabilities is kept in a subservient role by her supervising teacher, whose behavior management is questionable, and the student teacher finds herself in increasingly difficult circumstances midway through her eight week assignment.

WHOSE CLASS IS THIS? Jane Lee
Precis. Part A: A former special education teacher now teaching a regular fourth grade class has a continuing battle with a student's mother, who is a former teacher and sometimes serves as a substitute in the same school, over instructional and behavior management issues, culminating in the mother's direct attempt to dictate a behavior management strategy.

Part B: The teacher sends a letter to the mother, reasserting her professional judgment and authority, and is subsequently paid an unexpected visit by the father, a new school board member, which further shakes her confidence.

THE GHOST OF SCHOOL YEARS PAST: Jeannette Sloan
Precis. Part A: A first-year special education teacher in an elementary school finds herself a social outsider among the faculty, is constantly compared by her aide and others to her highly esteemed predecessor, who has returned to the university for a graduate degree, and eventually observes that her aide is not only usurping her authority in behavior management but questioning her decisions in discussions with other faculty.

Part B: The teacher confronts her aide, but subsequently discovers that her predecessor not only continues to influence her aide through frequent phone conversations but will be completing a practicum assignment in the school.

WINNIE: Patty Gray
Precis. Part A: A second-year teacher of at-risk first graders has particular problems with the behavior of one of her students, particularly his talking out and calling her name, and obtains help from a consulting teacher to develop a management plan, but she is not successful in resolving the problem by the Christmas holidays.

Part B: After school resumes in January, the teacher continues her efforts to resolve the child's behavior problems, including new strategies designed with the help of the consulting teacher, but she finds that the other students are beginning to imitate both him and her responses to him, and by the end of the school year she still has not found a solution.

YOU HAD BETTER GET ON THEM: Bob Winters
Precis. A teacher with formal preparation in early childhood special education assumes a position teaching middle school students with mild mental retardation and gradually looses all semblance of classroom control, ultimately lashing out at the students with unprofessional language and being confronted by the principal about his behavior.

Preface

The typical instructor's manual for the typical textbook is highly predictable in content, as it assumes that the course will be taught using traditional didactic procedures. MANAGING CLASSROOM BEHAVIOR: A REFLECTIVE CASE-BASED APPROACH is not a typical text, and its use requires that the instructor break the mold of traditional instruction. This manual is necessarily somewhat different in focus from those that accompany purely expository textbooks. Our purpose is to give you four things that we feel are critical to your success: (1) a conceptual orientation to the case method of teaching, (2) suggestions for using our text to design a case-based course and for how you might go about teaching cases, (3) the completion (Part B) of cases for which the students' text includes only Part A, and (4) notes on the cases included in our text which will help you in preparing to teach them. Please note that we have included in the Table of Contents and at the beginning of Part IV a precis for each case to help you find more quickly and remember the cases in which you are most interested.

A major purpose of case-based teaching is to get students highly involved, both cognitively and affectively, in descriptions of real-world problems and their solution. Thus, successful case-based teaching depends on stimulating classroom dialogue--not just student-instructor dialogue, but dialogue among students and within students and the instructor as well. Questioning oneself and others and searching together for fresh and productive questions and answers are the essential processes of teaching with cases. We and our students have found these teaching processes extremely rewarding, and we invite you to explore the case approach to teaching with us.

Like nearly everything else that is exciting and rewarding, teaching with cases requires study and practice. For most people, it is not a "snap." It requires a substantial investment of time and effort in preparation and careful management of classroom events. The return on this investment, however, can be enormous for both students and instructor. This manual provides a brief orientation and suggestions for getting started in a case-based approach to teaching behavior management using our text. If case-based teaching is new to you, however, we urge you to read widely from the works included in our references.

We wish to acknowledge with thanks the teachers who shared their experiences with us so that we could prepare the cases. Unfortunately, they and the other individuals involved in the cases must remain anonymous. We express our great appreciation for the support we received from the University of Virginia's Commonwealth Center for the Education of Teachers and its director, Robert F. McNergney. We are grateful to Karen E. Santos of James Madison University for giving us many helpful suggestions for preparation of this manual.

J. M. K.
M. P. M.
D. G. N.
S. C. T.
D. P. H.

Part I. Teaching by the Case Method: Orientation

Current Conceptualizations of Teacher Education

Until recently research on teaching in general education has been dominated by the search for relationships between teacher behavior and student outcomes. The methodology used by such researchers has involved the observation and coding of relatively specific teacher behaviors during instruction. The researcher then correlates these behaviors with some measure of student performance, for example, on-task behavior in the classroom or achievement test scores. Referred to as process-product research, this work has generated a number of consistent findings. Students whose performance is higher are more likely to have teachers who:

> structure the learning; proceed in small steps at a brisk pace; give detailed and redundant instructions and explanations; provide many examples; ask a large number of questions and corrections, particularly in the initial stages of learning new material; have a student success rate of 80% or higher in initial learning; divide seatwork assignments into smaller assignments; and provide for continued student practice so that students have a success rate of 90%-100% and become rapid, confident, and firm. (Rosenshine, 1983, pp. 336-337)

Although there have not been as many process-product studies on children with disabilities, the results have been generally similar (Larrivee, 1985). Furthermore, the notion of isolating specific teacher behaviors that correlate with student outcomes fits well with special education's traditional emphasis on competency-based instruction and behavioristic principles. Special educators have long held the notion that observable behaviors of teachers and students are the only useful tools and criteria for ensuring student success. During the heyday of competency-based teacher preparation in the 1960s and 1970s, special educators were among the strongest advocates of training preservice teachers to exhibit observable behaviors believed to result in academic and behavioral progress for students. And special educators have always been attracted to behaviorism because it has often resulted in positive changes for students with some very difficult behavioral problems.

Problems With the Process-Product/Competency-Based Behavioristic Orientation to Teacher Education

It is our contention that, although the process-product/competency-based, behavioristic legacy has served special education well, it can lead to an unduly narrow conceptualization of teacher education programming for handicapped students. First, there are inherent limitations in the process-product research paradigm. Process-product researchers have generally framed the problem to be studied as one of how to explain changes in student behavior based on the influence of teacher behavior. Some teacher behaviors, however, could be the result of student behaviors rather than vice versa. Several years ago, researchers in developmental psychology pointed out the problem of assuming that the causal chain between parent and child behavior always flows from the former to the latter (Bell & Harper, 1977). They noted that parent-child interaction is best characterized as reciprocal. That the relationship between teacher and student behavior is also reciprocal is extremely likely.

Second, teacher educators have sometimes misinterpreted such an approach as meaning that one should adopt an extremely algorithmic view of how to prepare future teachers. Train teachers to do more of x, y, z, and this will result in better student behavior. Even assuming that we knew what all the critical xs, ys, and zs were, which we do not, this approach fails to appreciate the complexity of what happens within classrooms. It is wishful thinking to presume that the relationship between teacher and student behavior is linear. Furthermore, an algorithmic model erroneously assumes that all children will react to teacher behavior in the same way all of the time. In other words, it ignores the heterogeneity between and within children that is the hallmark of children with mild disabilities.

Third, by adopting such an approach, some teacher educators have focused on teacher behavior to the relative neglect of teacher thinking. This oversight has occurred despite the fact that even the "grandfather" of the process-product paradigm, N. L. Gage has called for "respect for teachers' thinking and flexibility" (Gage & Needels, 1989, p. 289).

The unfortunate upshot of (a) focusing almost exclusively on the teacher's influence on the student, (b) approaching teacher behavior algorithmically, and (c) ignoring the thinking of teachers is the reinforcement of the notion of the behaviorist as an automaton--an unthinking, unfeeling dispenser of rewards and punishments. Effective teachers of children with disabilities must possess an armamentarium of behavior management techniques. They must approach children with a solid understanding of behavioral principles. At the same time, however, they need to be reflective in their administration of such principles. They need to recognize that some behavioral techniques do not work all of the time with all of the students. One often hears the complaint from teachers that research rarely provides definitive direction on how to treat specific problems. Another variation on this charge is that one can always find some piece of research to support whatever one wants to do. Although some of this ambiguity may be explained by methodological problems contained in some of the research being cited, we suspect that a fair share of it occurs because of contextual factors. That is, some educational treatments are better for certain problems under certain conditions. What works with one student under certain conditions probably does not work for all students. Parsing out the contextual factors so that one arrives as efficiently as possible at the best treatment approach for a particular problem with a particular student requires a sophisticated degree of decision making on the part of the teacher. Teachers must be able to make informed decisions about a number of things. For example, they need to decide what might be causing a particular behavior, which behavioral techniques might work, and whether a technique, once implemented, is working.

Teaching as a Reflective Activity: The Reflective Behaviorist

In general education, a movement away from an algorithmic toward a more cognitive view of teaching has already begun. Clark and Lampert (1986), for example, have noted the contextual, interactive, and speculative nature of teaching. Teachers make decisions that are situation-specific, they engage in reciprocal interactions with their students, and they cannot predict ahead of time the outcome of much of what they do. Another way of putting this is that teaching requires decision making in an ill-structured domain (Spiro, Vispoel, Schmitz, Samarapungavan, & Boerger, 1987). For Spiro et al., an ill-structured domain is characterized by prior knowledge or experience that is not easily translated into what one should do in the future. In other words, in teaching, the ability to transfer what one has learned in one situation into principles for action in another situation is not always easily accomplished. As evidence for this difficulty in transfer, Spiro et al. have noted:

The conditions for applying old knowledge are subject to considerable variability, and that variability in turn requires flexibility of response. Monolithic representations of knowledge will too often leave their holders facing situations for which their rigid "plaster-casts" simply do not fit. The result is the often heard complaint of students: "We weren't taught that." By which they mean that they weren't taught exactly that. They lack the ability to use their knowledge in new ways, the ability to think for themselves. (pp. 180-181)

With specific regard to students with behavior problems, there has been little movement toward a more reflective teaching approach. Some have advocated the use of cognitive behavior modification with these students, but this is the combining of cognitive and behavioral principles by the child. What we are advocating is that the teacher adopt a more reflective disposition while operating under behavioristic principles. Although the notion of a reflective behaviorist may seem an oxymoron to some, to us it is the essence of what it takes to be an effective manager of students with behavior problems.

The Value of Cases

Toward the goal of preparing teachers who are reflective managers of student behavior, we have adopted a case method approach to instruction. In this regard, we follow in the footsteps of several others who have recommended the case method of instruction in teacher education, e.g., Carter and Unkelsbay (1989), Kleinfeld (1988), Merseth (1991), Morine-Dershimer (1991), Shulman (1986), Silverman, Welty, and Lyon (1992), Spiro et al. (1987). And these teacher educators, in turn, owe a great debt to the law and business schools, which have a long history of using the case method.

Although teacher educators who advocate a case method have not focused as specifically on behavior management of mildly handicapped students in mainstream classrooms as we have in Managing classroom behavior: A case-method approach, we are indebted to their providing the rationale for using the case method to enhance teachers' problem-solving abilities. Shulman (1986), for example, has persuasively argued that the case method promotes strategic knowledge--the ability to decide what to do when confronted with situations or problems wherein "principles collide and no simple solution is possible" (p. 13). He gives the example of Rowe's (1974) conclusions regarding wait-time that dictate that longer wait-times lead to higher levels of cognition conflicting with Kounin's (1970) research indicating that slow-paced instruction results in an increase in discipline problems. A teacher confronted with these two apparently contradictory sets of findings must decide which one fits his or her particular situation.

Merseth (1991) has provided a similar rationale for using a case method in teacher preparation:

This new conceptualization of teacher knowledge also recognizes that teaching is a field organized around human interaction under the strong influence of specific contexts. It does matter what one is teaching, to whom, under what conditions. Hence, accurate prediction as a result of dispassionate and pure deduction is not likely.

Rather, teaching is seen as an endeavor that functions in situations where neither universal laws nor total chaos prevails, where neither deduction nor induction reigns supreme, and where certain principles in teaching do exist but do not ground every teaching action. Seen in this way, teacher knowledge falls on a new middle ground.

It is here, in this middle ground, that the case for cases is most powerful. To choose cases as a pedagogy is to embrace a belief that while theoretic principles may be important and must be learned by those who teach, simply knowing a principle is of little use. Cases assume that what we need are teachers who are able to apply principles and even to devise new ones (Kennedy, 1987; Schon, 1987). (p.13)

In many ways, those who champion a case method are attempting to teach novices to think more like those with more experience and expertise. They see a case method as a way of speeding up the socialization process. For several years, James Boyd White, a law professor, has delivered a speech to entering law school students that emphasizes the use of cases in training the "legal mind." Much of what he says would hold for the education profession. One could substitute the word "teacher" for "lawyer" and "education" for "law" in the following quote and depict our view of the value of using cases in teacher education:

Let me suggest that you regard the law, not as a set of rules to be memorized, but as an activity, as something that people do with their minds and with each other as they act in relation both to a body of authoritative legal material and to the circumstances and events of the actual world. The law is a set of social and intellectual practices that defines a universe or culture in which you will learn to function.... Our primary aim is not to transmit information to you but to help you learn how to do what it is that lawyers do with the problems that come to them....

Of course the law as an activity can and should be studied...from the point of view of other disciplines.... But in studying the law in such ways one is functioning, not as a lawyer, but as an anthropologist, as a historian, and so forth. What is peculiar and central to your experience both in law school and beyond is that you learn how to participate in this activity, not as an academic, but as a legal mind....

A[n] analogy [to learning law] may be learning a language. One must of course learn the rules of grammar and the meaning of terms, but to know those things is not to know how to speak the language. That knowledge comes only with use. (White, 1985, pp. 52-53)

Evidence for the Value of Cases

But what is the evidence that the case method will actually result in teachers being better problem solvers and decision makers? Unfortunately, there is surprisingly little methodologically sound research on the use of cases in law, business, or teacher education. In one of the first well-controlled investigations of using cases in teacher preparation, Kleinfeld (1991) randomly divided students in a course on Diagnosis and Evaluation of Learning into a group taught by a case method and a control group taught by discussion of readings and practical exercises. She found that cases led to a greater ability to analyze an educational problem and a tendency for students to be more likely to view teachers as decision-making professionals.

Some of the most recent research in cognitive science can be used as indirect evidence for the potential value of using cases in teacher education. Many cognitive psychologists are now promoting the idea that individuals do not learn how to solve problems of everyday life in a vacuum. These theorists draw a distinction between how people solve problems in practical situations and how they solve them under more abstract situations. Rogoff (1984) notes that in everyday life action drives thought. People do not use formalistic thinking to solve everyday problems. Systematic and precise thinking may actually be more inefficient in solving practical problems. As Lave (1988) has found, people do not use formal mathematical operations when faced with a problem such as: Fix a serving of cottage cheese equivalent to three-quarters of two-thirds of a cup. Instead, they measure two-thirds of a cup, pour it out, and then take out three-quarters of it by hand.

Brown, Collins, and Duguid (1989) have forwarded the theory of "situated cognition" to refer to the idea that how people solve problems cannot be divorced from the context in which the problem occurs. The closely related concept of "cognitive apprenticeship" (Collins, Brown, & Newman, 1989) is also applicable as a rationale for the use of cases in teacher preparation. Cognitive apprenticeship refers to the notion that people learn best when they learn as close to the context as possible under the tutelage of experts whom they can model. Discussing cases that require solutions to real problems encountered by real teachers, although a step removed from actually having to solve the problems in the natural setting, should be more helpful in making teachers better problem solvers than teachers trained through traditional lecture and discussion formats. Cases provide a narrative of teachers in action. Discussing cases provides a forum for preservice teachers to try out ideas and potential solutions before actually being faced with making those decisions under fire in the classroom. For the inservice teacher, discussing cases provides the opportunity to hone their decision making skills. In this way, then, a case method can serve as a bridge between academia and the classroom.

A further benefit of using a case method pertains to the social aspect of discussing cases. Brown et al. (1989) and Lave and Wenger (in preparation) (cited in Brown et al.) pointed out that much can be gained from working together to solve problems:

> Within a culture, ideas are exchanged and modified and belief systems developed and appropriated through conversation and narratives.... Though they are often anathema to traditional schooling, they are an essential component of social interaction and, thus, of learning....
>
> An intriguing role in learning is played by "legitimate peripheral participation," where people who are not taking part directly in a particular activity learn a great deal from their legitimate position on the periphery (Lave & Wenger, in preparation). It is a mistake to think that important discourse in learning is always direct and declarative. This peripheral participation is particularly important for people entering the culture [italics added]. They need to observe how practitioners at various levels behave and talk to get a sense of how expertise is manifest in conversation and other activities. (Brown, Collins, & Duguid, 1989, p. 40)

The Future of Cases

Assuming that teaching by a case method leads to teachers who are better problem solvers and more reflective, there has been much speculation about whether the use of cases will catch on in teacher education. Although there is evidence of an increase in the use of cases, the movement is gradual (White & McNergney, 1991). The widespread adoption of cases in law and business, however, took several years to happen, and most innovations in education do not occur overnight. Morine-Dershimer (1991) believes the case method is well positioned to be widely adopted because it has the flexibility to fit with the values of the major orientations in teacher education (Feiman-Nemser, 1990; Zeichner & Liston, 1990). She notes that although a case method should appeal most to teacher educators who hold a practical orientation, those from other philosophical persuasions (i.e., academic, technical skills, critical/social, personal/developmental) should find nothing objectionable in using cases.

Though we are encouraged by our own experiences in using a case method, we hasten to point out that much more research is needed on the utility of this approach. In addition to needing research on the fundamental question of whether using cases leads to better problem solving and more reflection, we need answers to a variety of other questions. For example, we have adopted the Harvard Business School model (Christensen, 1987) of relatively brief (about 2,000 words) cases that end at the point at which a teacher needs to make a decision. Kleinfeld (1988), on the other hand, uses cases that are much longer and more complete. An obvious question pertains to which approach is better for which purposes. It is also interesting to consider the best way to sequence the presentation of cases. For example, following the logic of situated cognition and cognitive apprenticeship whereby action drives thinking, it might make more sense for students to read and discuss cases prior to reading the theoretical foundations of a field. In our text, we have presented the cases after the theoretical material, believing that students will derive more benefit from the cases if they have a repertoire of basic concepts to which they can refer as they read the cases. These and other questions beg for research.

Part II. Suggestions for Using This Text

Our experience and observation of our university colleagues indicates that few texts, if any, are used in the same way by all instructors who adopt it. This text, we believe, is likely to be used in a greater variety of ways than most. Case-based teaching demands considerable flexibility and creativity in designing courses and devising teaching strategies. We offer several suggestions for how you might organize a case-based course and use this text. We recognize, however, that there are many other ways to teach such a course and use the text and that you will need to consider the context in which you teach, the characteristics of your students, the resources at your disposal, and your own instructional proclivities.

Using the Chapters and Cases

The text provides expository chapters on various topics and principles, followed by a series of cases. The cases are not matched to specific chapters, nor did we intend to provide a case to illustrate every possible point of discussion in the chapters. Rather, we collected a variety of cases that lend themselves to a wide range of emphases and that offer points for discussion related to numerous principles and practices. Which cases are best used in combination with which chapters? In our view, there is not a single answer to this question. We believe that you must answer this question for yourself after you have read the chapters, the cases, and the teaching notes for the cases, as important issues related to each chapter are raised by several different cases.

You will, probably, want students to read all seven chapters of the text. You may decide not to teach all the cases, however, depending on how many instructional hours are available to you in the term and how many other activities besides case analysis you include in your course requirements. The very brief summaries of the cases included in the table of contents and preceding Part IV are intended to help you make selections of the cases you think would be best for your students. We do not suggest that you teach the cases in any particular order; choose a sequence that is best for the students in your class.

As Part I of this manual suggests, case-based teaching can be structured in many ways to enhance more traditional didactic instruction. You will need to consider several different options for using the chapters of the text in combination with the cases. Perhaps you will want to assign and discuss all seven chapters prior to teaching any cases. More likely, you will want to alternate chapters and cases. Should cases be taught after students have read chapters, or should chapters be assigned following students' study of cases? Will the chapters be more understandable to students after they have studied cases or vice versa? We do not know, and we--like others who are engaged in case-based teaching--are continuing to experiment with different tactics for making cases and more prescriptive materials work better in combination.

Selecting Course Structure and Requirements

A course in which this text might be used could be structured in a variety of ways. We recommend putting considerable emphasis on participating in class discussions and writing answers to questions about cases, as these are the heart of case teaching. Ordinarily, we have required attending and participating in class discussions, reading the chapters in the text and selected journal articles that amplify certain principles or procedures, writing answers to study questions about assigned cases prior to discussion (or answers to reflection questions about cases we have discussed), participating in a focus group that becomes "expert" on a particular management strategy and creates a useful product to share with all class members, and writing a case based on personal experience. We have not tested students on the text material or other readings, although this is certainly an option to consider. Some of these course requirements are "standard" for most instructors; others may require some explanation. Following is a description of possible course requirements, all of which we explain in more detail.

1. <u>Attendance and Participation</u>. Students are expected to attend class regularly and to participate regularly in analysis of cases as both listener and contributor in class discussions.

2. <u>Readings</u>. Readings will be assigned for most class sessions. The text is intended primarily as a resource for case analysis and group work, but specific reading assignments will be made from it and each chapter will be discussed in class. Additional readings may also be assigned, and students are expected to find and read materials related to their work in a focus group.

3. <u>Written Answers to Study or Reflection Questions on Cases</u>. A case will be discussed each week. Students are expected to read each case carefully, consult the text and other professional literature for guidance in analyzing the case, and contribute to class discussion of the case. Study questions will be provided for most of the cases. For some cases, students will be expected to prepare written answers to the study questions before the class session in which the case is discussed (i.e., written answers are due at the beginning of class). Some class sessions devoted to discussion of a case will end with students writing their reflections on the case in the light of the points brought out during its discussion. No tests or quizzes will be given, but graders will look for information referenced to readings in discussions and written work.

4. <u>Participation in a Focus Group</u>. Each student will be part of a small focus group, the purpose of which is to (a) assemble detailed information from the research and professional literatures regarding a specific behavior management strategy and make it available to all members of the class in a readily accessible form and (b) serve as a "panel of experts" in case discussions in which the strategy they are researching is an issue. Contributions to class by the focus group will be part of the final grade, with some points allocated by the instructor and some points determined by peer ratings.

5. <u>Written Case</u>. Each student will develop a written case suitable for analysis and teaching (these cases will not be used in the class). The case will be written in stages (i.e., ungraded drafts) over the course of the semester, with guidance and periodic feedback from the instructor or graduate assistants on each draft, and must be drawn from the student's actual experience with a behavior management problem or on an in-depth interview with a teacher regarding a behavior management problem. Only the final draft of the case will be graded.

Attendance and Participation

In our experience, students respond well to the attendance and participation requirement and to its being a significant part of the course grade when we describe the case method of teaching to them and emphasize the importance of each student's regular participation. We structure the grading criteria to include a small number of points for attending and participating (at some minimal level) in each class session.

Readings

We have not spent much time discussing the chapters in the text or other readings aside from the context of particular cases. However, we have found it helpful to assign specific chapters to be read by specific dates and to encourage students to ask questions about the text chapters. We emphasize to students that we expect them to make specific references to the text material and other readings when we are discussing cases or they are writing answers to study or reflection questions. Our hope is that students will demonstrate their understanding of what they have read by applying it to real-world problems.

Written Answers to Study and Reflection Questions

Students should come to class having read and studied the case to be discussed. We typically assign a case one week in advance. For most cases, particularly early in the semester, we provide study questions to help students focus in on major issues. We usually require students to write out their answers and turn them in. Sometimes we ask students to write answers to "reflection" questions during the last 10 to 20 minutes of class after we have discussed the case. When we teach a case with Parts A and B, we assign students to read Part A a week in advance of our discussion, then give them Part B to read in class after we have discussed Part A.

Written answers to study questions help students prepare for class discussions. The feedback we have received from our students is that they do not see study questions as busy work; the questions help them focus on particular aspects of the case and see the issues in the case differently than they might have without questions to guide them. Writing out their answers helps students think through the issues and provides a beginning point for deeper analysis.

The purpose of asking students to write answers to reflection questions following the discussion of a case is to assess (and help them assess) the way their thinking about the case has changed. We always see a case from a new perspective after teaching it; we believe students see it differently as well. Writing about that change in perspective--articulating how and why the discussion altered their analysis of events--adds to the richness of case study.

Participation in a Focus Group

Our feeling is that students in a course in behavior management should become well acquainted with specific techniques and strategies. The text is not designed to give students in-depth information regarding specific methods of behavior management; it offers a reflective perspective, sketches basic principles, and provides cases for discussion of the application of those principles while maintaining that perspective. One vehicle for engaging students in reading current professional literature and helping them obtain greater knowledge of specific methods of behavior management is to require their working in small groups. We have required students to participate in small "focus" groups of 3 to 5 students. The group must work cooperatively to focus on a specific intervention strategy and create a product useful to themselves and their classmates.

9

At the initial class session in which we discuss course requirements, we distribute a description of how we want the focus groups to work. The following is an example of how we explain the structure and purpose of the focus groups.

Points to Remember in Working in Your Focus Group

1. The main idea of the focus group is to provide up-to-date, accurate, and useful information to the class regarding a specific behavior management technique or strategy. You will need to search out recent studies as well as "classic" articles about the procedure you have chosen.

2. You must include as part of your product a full bibliographic listing of the sources you used to prepare your guidelines for practice. (Use the reference lists in your textbook as a guide for preparing your reference list.) Anyone using your product should be able to find the sources on which your suggestions, conclusions, and cautions are based.

3. Your product should be a handy, practical, and research-based guide for other teachers. It should be based to the greatest extent possible on a body of careful research. Professional books and journals in special education and psychology should be your primary sources.

   a. It should include the rationale for the procedure--a simple and clear explanation of the principles that make it work.

   b. It should present clearly and succinctly the major Dos and Don'ts of using the procedure, based on the research literature.

   c. It should include qualifying statements (e.g., What are the major indicators and contraindicators that the procedure might be the procedure of choice? What are the limitations of the procedure?).

4. When we are discussing cases in class, look for opportunities to raise questions about and suggest uses of, or guidelines for the use of, the technique you have chosen.

The number and size of the focus groups will depend on the enrollment in your course. We have found that six is a workable number and that three to five is the ideal number of students per group. You may wish to give students a list of possible topics for the focus groups and ask them to indicate their preferences. Following are six topics that we once used with a class of 18 students; you may consider many other topics as well.

CONTINGENCY CONTRACTS:	Preparing and administering behavioral and academic contracts having students as signatories.
DIFFERENTIAL REINFORCEMENT:	Finding the best means of programming positive reinforcement for appropriate behavior as a means of decreasing problems behavior (e.g., differential reinforcement of other behavior, or DRO).
TIME OUT:	Setting up time out contingencies and establishing guidelines for placing students in and releasing them from time out.
TOKEN REWARD SYSTEMS:	Designing, acquiring, and implementing a reward system in which tokens are exchanged for back-up reinforcers.
SELF-MONITORING:	Planning and implementing procedures for getting students to monitor their own behavior or academic progress.
SOCIAL SKILLS TRAINING:	Identifying specific behavior required for social acceptance by peers and adults and designing procedures for teaching these skills.

We have found it helpful to give students general information about the focus groups and specific suggestions for where they might start in locating relevant publications. Following is an example of what we have provided.

Sources of Information for Focus Groups

Note on Sharing Information Sources

The focus groups are not set up as a competitive exercise. Nothing is to be lost and much is to be gained by sharing sources of information with your classmates. Please be considerate of others and work together to help each focus group find the best sources.

General Sources of Information

Journals. Many professional journals in education and psychology carry articles on specific behavior management procedures. Indexes such as Education Index, Cumulative Index of Journals in Education, and Psychological Abstracts are useful. Some journals publish periodic indexes of their contents that are very helpful in locating material on specific topics; most include tables of contents that can be scanned quickly for articles on specific topics. One of the best ways of getting leads on good articles is to locate a recent one on a particular topic and examine the reference citations. Some of the journal titles that you may find particularly important are:

> Behavior Modification
> Behavioral Disorders
> Education and Treatment of Children
> Journal of Applied Behavior Analysis
> Journal of Behavioral Education

Books. Many books on the general topic of behavior management are good sources of information about specific management techniques. Use the card catalog and reference citations in books you already have or know about (don't forget your text for this course!) to seek out those that are most helpful. Following are some titles that you may find particularly useful:

Emmer, E. T., Evertson, C. M., Sanford, J. P., Clements, B. S., & Worsham, M. E. (1989). Classroom management for secondary teachers (2nd ed.). Boston: Allyn & Bacon.

Jones, V. F., & Jones, L. S. (1990). Comprehensive classroom management: Motivating and managing students (3rd ed.). Boston: Allyn & Bacon.

Kerr, M. M., & Nelson, C. M. (1989). Strategies for managing behavior problems in the classroom (2nd ed.). Columbus, OH: Merrill/Macmillan.

Kerr, M. M., Nelson, C. M., & Lambert, D. L. (1987). Helping adolescents with learning and behavior problems. Columbus, OH: Merrill/Macmillan.

Morgan, D. P., & Jenson, W. R. (1988). Teaching behaviorally disordered students: Preferred practices. Columbus, OH: Merrill/Macmillan.

O'Leary, K. D., & O'Leary, S. G. (1977). Classroom management: The successful use of behavior modification (2nd ed.). New York: Pergamon.

References Specific to Focus Group Topics

Following are two reference citations for each of the focus topics. Some are recent, some are "classics;" some are reviews or descriptions of techniques, some are research studies. Together, they represent the range of old, new, descriptive, and experimental literature on which your focus group should draw.

CONTINGENCY CONTRACTS

Homme, L. (1969). How to use contingency contracting in the classroom. Champaign, IL: Research Press.

Kelly, M. L., & Stokes, T. F. (1982). Contingency contracting with disadvantaged youths: Improving classroom performance. Journal of Applied Behavior Analysis, 15, 447-454.

DIFFERENTIAL REINFORCEMENT

Deitz, D. E. D., & Repp, A. C. (1983). Reducing behavior through reinforcement. Exceptional Education Quarterly, 3(4), 34-46.

Repp, A. C., Barton, L. E., & Brulle, A. R. (1983). A comparison of two procedures for programming the differential reinforcement of other behaviors. Journal of Applied Behavior Analysis, 16, 435-445.

TIME OUT

Foxx, R. M., & Shapiro, S. T. (1978). The timeout ribbon: A nonexclusionary timeout procedure. Journal of Applied Behavior Analysis, 11, 125-136.

Nelson, C. M., & Rutherford, R. B. (1983). Timeout revisited: Guidelines for its use in special education. Exceptional Education Quarterly, 3(4), 56-67.

TOKEN REINFORCEMENT

O'Leary, K. D., & Becker, W. C. (1967). Behavior modification of an adjustment class: A token reinforcement program. Exceptional Children, 33, 637-642.

O'Leary, K. D., & Drabman, R. (1971). Token reinforcement in the classroom: A review. Psychological Bulletin, 75, 379-398.

SELF-MONITORING

De Haas-Warner, S. J. (1991). Effects of self-monitoring on preschoolers' on-task behavior: A pilot study. Topics in Early Childhood Special Education, 11(2), 59-73.

Lloyd, J. W., Landrum, T. J., & Hallahan, D. P. (1991). Self-monitoring applications for classroom intervention. In G. Stoner, M. R. Shinn, & H. M. Walker (Eds.), Interventions for achievement and behavior problems (pp. 201-213). Silver Spring, MD: National Association of School Psychologists.

SOCIAL SKILLS

Sabornie, E. J. (1991). Measuring and teaching social skills in the mainstream. In G. Stoner, M.R. Shinn, & H. M. Walker (Eds.), Interventions for achievement and behavior problems (pp. 161-177). Silver Spring, MD: National Association of School Psychologists.

Whalen, C. K., & Henker, B. (1991). Social impact of stimulant treatment for hyperactive children. Journal of Learning Disabilities, 24, 231-241.

Focus groups must start their work early in the term if they are to be of maximum benefit. Furthermore, we have found it necessary to assign specific tasks and plan for reports and discussion at specific points in the course schedule. Several of our class sessions are devoted entirely to focus group reports and discussion rather than case analysis. Following are examples of how you might structure an initial assignment for focus groups early in the term and how you might use focus groups to connect what they are reading and discovering in the professional literature to the cases they are analyzing.

Initial Focus Group Assignment

Work with the other two members of your group to find, read, and discuss several initial sources of information on your topic. Come to class ready to answer (as a group) questions about your topic for 15 to 20 minutes. You should be ready to respond to the following and to questions from your classmates and instructor.

1. What sources of information have you turned up to date? What has been your most successful search strategy?

2. What are the most important features or dimensions of your management strategy that you have discovered during the past week?

3. Of the cases we have studied so far, which do you think provides the best opportunity for application of your management strategy? Why?

Focus Group Assignment # 2

Work with the other members of your focus group to prepare a 15 to 20 minute report in which all three of you participate. Your presentation should address the following:

1. Of the cases we have studied so far, choose the one that you think provides the best opportunity for using your management strategy. What led you to believe that this case lends itself best to the use of your strategy (i.e., what are the indications that the strategy might work well)?

2. Give as many specifics as you can about how you would implement your strategy with the case you have chosen. That is, provide a step-by-step plan for using the strategy to manage the specific problem(s) as you understand it(them).

3. What case do you see as particularly ill-suited to the use of your strategy? Why would your strategy not be a good choice for that case?

Be prepared to answer questions from other students and the instructors. Please plan your presentation carefully to make sure that you do not exceed the 20 minute time limit.

The timing and pacing of the focus groups is something you will have to consider carefully. You will also need to consider whether you want students to share drafts of their products with you before turning in the final draft; we suggest that you do this. You may also want to have each group's draft product critiqued by another focus group.

The nature and quality of the products created by our focus groups has varied tremendously. Creativity, thoroughness in exploring the topic, and access to work processing equipment or other readily available technology can result in student's sharing very helpful products. The products are likely to be primarily print media, but they need not be exclusively so. We offer brief descriptions of two products shared in one of our classes that in our judgment--and in the judgment of our students' classmates--were among the best.

1.   "TIME OUT "Tips for Teachers"--a single 8.5" x 11" sheet folded into thirds to form a flyer or pamphlet and including accurate and succinct statements about what time out is, what it is not, dos and don'ts for using time out and a listing of information resources.

2.   SELF-MONITORING KIT--A brief paper (5 pages) describing how self-monitoring can be used to improve task attention, including materials needed, basic training procedure, weaning procedure, evaluation, recording forms, references for further information, and an audio tape with recorded beeps (one of the essential components that many teachers find a difficult to find or make).

Written Case

Writing a case based on their own experience, students tell us, helps them think through what happened, their feelings about the events, and what they might have done differently. Before students begin writing their own case, they should have read and analyzed several cases in the text. Furthermore, it may be very helpful to ask students to examine a case using the suggestions in our "Notes on Writing Cases" before they begin writing their own. As they read cases and begin writing their own, students should discover the subtle but essential features of a good case. By writing their own cases, students gain additional insights into the cases of others as well. Understanding how a good case is written should contribute to students' ability to be reflective and analytical in approaching behavior management problems.

Some of our students have had very limited classroom experience, and we have asked these students to interview an experienced teacher regarding a behavior management incident about which the student can write a case. Ideally, the teacher will work with the student, reading and commenting on at least one draft to help the student understand the importance of certain events and the teacher's feelings about them.

A good case is not something that can be composed easily or quickly. Writing a case is a difficult assignment, and we have found it important to require that students hand in several drafts and obtain feedback on each. We provide feedback on each draft, but we grade only the final draft. The number of drafts required will depend to some extent on the level of experience and writing abilities of your students. You might have students begin by turning in a draft of the beginning paragraphs rather than a draft of the entire case. If you choose to have your students write a case as one of the course requirements, you might consider providing them an outline of major points similar to the following, which we have used.

Notes on Writing Cases

I.   What a case is: a narrative account of a behavior management problem that presents a dilemma for resolution by the reader

    A.   What a case should do

        1.   represent the reality of the problem and its context as completely and accurately as possible

        2.   offer no simulations, only personal recollections that will stimulate discussion and analysis at multiple levels of abstraction

    B.   Characteristics of a useful case

        1.   highlights issues in a troubling situation and identifies various dimensions of the problem (e.g., ethical, pedagogical, political, & policy issues)

        2.   frames problems in productive ways (i.e., that allow analysis)

        3.   facilitates analysis of multiple causal factors

        4.   suggests options (both obvious and subtle) for approaching the problem

        5.   suggests risks, ramifications, and possible consequences of alternative courses of action

        6.   deals with cognitive and affective aspects of the problem

    C.   Choosing what to write about

        1.   any narrative can be turned into a case if it includes description of:
            a.   a problem or dilemma in sufficient detail
            b.   a teacher's actions
            c.   what happened as a result of the teacher's actions
            d.   the teacher's perceptions and reflections on the problem and what happened

        2.   must describe an actual situation, not hypothetical

        3.   must present a dilemma

        4.   must present complex situation (more complex problem than may be immediately apparent)

        5.   teacher must be individual responsible for action

        6.   must generate more than one possible solution

        7.   may be drawn from your own experience (present or past) or the experience of someone you interview in depth

II.   Writing a case

    A.   Evaluation of initial idea

        1.   Are you able to present case completely and honestly?
        2.   Does case present a sensitive or important issue?
        3.   Might writing the case cause anyone harm?
            a.   use pseudonyms
            b.   mask identities without distorting important facts

    B.   Gathering information and planning a case

        1.   Can you supply complete information?
        2.   Are you maintaining an open mind and reflecting different perspectives?
        3.   How are you ensuring an accurate chronology?
        4.   What will you include?
        5.   Do the incidents hold together as a story?

    C.   Parts of the case

        1.   Introduction
            a.   make it action-oriented
            b.   create a setting
        2.   Initial exposition--unfolding the background
        3.   Development--fleshing out the issues
        4.   Summary or conclusion--posing dilemma or question regarding future action

    D.   Drafting the case

        1.   usually in past tense
        2.   avoid dating the incidents
        3.   think of the case as a "story"
            a.   provide picture of main character(s)
            b.   describe main events and characters' reactions
            c.   build clear depiction of problem or conflict
            d.   describe attempted resolutions
            e.   keep main point or theme clearly in mind
        4.   possible formats or literary devices
            a.   first person or third person narrative
            b.   interview responses
            c.   stage play
            d.   diary

    E.   Ethics of writing cases

        1.   stay close enough to actual details to avoid misrepresentation of problem
        2.   change names and locations (and perhaps genders) to protect identities of characters and institutions
        3.   obtain signed release from interviewee

We recommend that you emphasize certain ethical issues in case writing. Confidentiality is beyond important--it is absolutely essential. Under no circumstances should any draft of the case reveal the identity of any individual who might suffer adverse or embarrassing consequences of the case being read by others.

Preparing to Teach a Case

Teaching a case requires a lot of preparation, compared to a lecture approach. This extensive preparation involves not only knowing the facts of the case well but understanding the nuances of the case and having a plan for helping students analyze characters, situations, and interactions. We have found teaching cases to be highly demanding and stimulating, in part because each time we teach a given case we discover new perspectives on a character, circumstance, or interaction. Each time we teach a case, particularly when we dissect the class discussion that it generated, we see new possibilities for teaching it.

One of the frustrating aspects of studying cases is that you would always like to have more information; no case includes all the bits of information that would be helpful. Students typically ask about various aspect of the case about which no information is given. They also want to know what happened next. We can provide only this suggestion for both instructor and students: work with the information you have, be sure that you attend carefully to all the information provided in the case, and be careful to state your assumptions when you go beyond that information in analyzing the case. As for what happened next--well, cases are like novels, in that readers must be left to speculate.

We have found two devices particularly helpful in preparing to teach a case: a case outline and a board outline. We provide an example of each for "WHAT YOU DON'T KNOW CAN HURT YOU! John McCullum." Our experience is that making the outlines oneself is extremely helpful and that no two instructors will prepare identical outlines.

Writing the Case Outline

The case outline provides us with a point-by-point, event-by-event summary of who was involved and what happened. Making our own outline helps us make certain that we have a clear understanding of who did what to whom, making us less likely to overlook a detail that may be important in analyzing the case. Following is an outline one of us made of "WHAT YOU DON'T KNOW CAN HURT YOU" prior to teaching.

Case outline, "WHAT YOU DON'T KNOW CAN HURT YOU! John McCullum"

I.   Characters

     A.   Teacher: John, student teacher

B. Students:

    1. Richard
        a. usually quiet
        b. low-achieving
        c. retained several times; larger & older than other students

    2. Chris
        a. high-achieving

C. Clinical instructor (supervising teacher)

D. Substitute teacher

E. Richard's English teacher from next room

F. Assistant Principal: Mr. Roberts

G. Class: 15 eighth graders

    1. 7 high-achieving
        a. one black female

    2. 8 low-achieving
        a. 5 talked, laughed, attempted to dominate class
        b. 7 black, 1 white male

    3. white students from upper middle-class neighborhoods; black students from relatively poor homes

H. Student passing in hall

II. Settings

A. Classroom

B. Hallway

C. Bike rack

D. Office

III. John's Background Experiences

A. With class

    1. accustomed to having complete freedom to plan
    2. only troublesome class

B.   With clinical instructor:

    1.   seldom if ever in class
    2.   typically gave students individual written assignments; little group work or direct instruction

C.   With Richard: any? (usually quiet)

IV.   John's Plans for Class

A.   Review for test in form of quiz show

B.   Use variety of instructional techniques

V.   Episodes

A.   Around quiz game (test), 7th period

    1.   John directs students to form groups of own choice
    2.   Groups self-select along racial and achievement lines
    2.   Argument erupts between Richard & Chris during game
    3.   John gets steps between students, returns to game
    3.   Hostile exchange occurs between Richard & Chris at class dismissal
    4.   John calls both students back
    5.   Chris complies, Richard runs

B.   Around bike rack after school that day

    1.   John wants to talk to Richard
    2.   Richard leaves
    3.   John submits disciplinary referral

C.   Around office next morning

    1.   John presents referral and walks Richard to office
    2.   < 30 min later John goes to office to copy, sees Richard
    3.   Richard makes threatening comments, John ignores
    4.   John leaves office, glances at Richard at water fountain
    5.   Richard says, "Don't be looking at me, boy."
    6.   John responds through clenched teeth

D.   Around Richard showing up for class that afternoon

    1.   Mr. Roberts had agreed to keep Richard in ISS
    2.   Richard quiet and low-key throughout class
    3.   John reminds Richard of detention; Richard says he has to catch bus
    4.   John says ok, but he must stay tomorrow

E. Around detention after school next afternoon

    1. Richard not in class; with Mr. Roberts in ISS
    2. Richard says that Mr. Roberts told him he had to come to detention
    3. John attempts to explain why he was given detention
    4. Richards' behavior becomes erratic
       a. refuses to be seated
       b. strikes objects in room with yardstick
    5. John sends students working on project to library
    6. John repeats explanation for referral; Richard responds with question, "How come Chris didn't get a referral?"
    7. John tries several more times to explain--referral not for fighting but for not coming when called
    8. Richard performs threatening rap lyrics; says he's going to tell vice-principal John attacked him; calls John names; drinks from bottle; wanders out of classroom
    9. John follows Richard out of classroom, explains he must stay in room during detention
    10. Richard precedes John into room, holds door
    11. John tries to work in classroom
    12. Richard sings loudly, John can't concentrate
    13. John gives Richard stern look
    14. Richard leaps from seat & confronts John (e.g., "You got a problem?")
    15. John senses danger, sees student walking in hall, goes into hallway and asks student to get teacher next door (Richard's English teacher)
    16. Teacher steps into classroom & sternly orders Richard to sit down
    17. Richard retaliates with sharp remarks
    18. Teacher goes to vice-principal
    19. Vice-principal tells teacher to release Richard
    20. John tells Richard he will report his behavior and refer him again
    21. Richard refuses to leave, believing John cannot refer him again if he stays
    22. John gives Richard permission to stay but reminds him he will be referred again

---

Planning Questions for Discussion

Preparing to teach a case requires one to plan a line of questioning. A critical requirement of teaching effectively with cases is asking questions that require higher level thinking. At some point in teaching a case, however, it may be important to get the facts of the case out with simpler questions (this is particularly likely to be important in teaching the first few cases with a group of students). Preparing to teach a case, then, requires one to plan a line of questioning. We have found it extremely important to write down questions we might ask, not only to clarify them in our own minds prior to teaching the case but to have as a ready reference while teaching. Often, the questions we prepare are tentative; typically, we prepare more questions than we have time to discuss and choose our line of questioning as the case analysis proceeds. We present the following example of questions one of us prepared for teaching, but we caution that a very different approach may be appropriate for other instructors and students.

Questions for "WHAT YOU DON'T KNOW CAN HURT YOU! John McCullum"

Sequence:

1. How would you describe the central problem--the biggest problem, the most important issue--in this case?

2. What additional problems do you see as part of the case?

3. To try to sort out just what happened in this case, let's review the people, places, background variables, and events.

   A. Who were the people (the "actors" or "players")?

   B. Let's list the places in which the case unfolded.

   C. What do we know about John's "history," his background experience with the people involved in the case?

   D. The events in this case unfolded in several distinct episodes over a period of days. Before we get into what happened in detail, let's get a thumbnail descriptions of these (five) episodes.

4. Now that we know how these episodes unfolded, we can see each is a possible point for intervention. Which one(s) do you think provide the best opportunity for John to address the central problem of this case?

5. What might John have done at (this) point that might have been more appropriate? How is your suggestion related to behavior principles?

6. Consider these 6 behavior principles:

   consequences
           stimulus control
   reinforcement
           positive
           negative
   extinction
   punishment
   contingency
   modeling

How was each of these involved in the (number) episode? How might each be applied more appropriately?

Other Possible Questions:

1. How would you characterize John (Richard) in his role as teacher (student)? The clinical instructor? What tells you what they were like (i.e., on what basis are you making that inference)?

2. Why did John want to try different techniques instead of following the lead of his clinical instructor? How did he set himself up for failure in the way he went about "experimenting?"

3. What aspects of the setting in which John was doing his student teaching do you see as positive or facilitative of his growth? How were these aspects of the setting facilitative (or not) of the growth of the students?

4. What do you think of John's efforts to explain and justify his own actions?

5. How do most student teachers learn instructional and behavior management techniques?

Wrap-up Summary (this is very tentative):

1. A major issue in this case was obtaining compliance--achieving stimulus control (in this case, so that students do what they're told or asked to do).

2. Achieving stimulus control and compliance depends on systematic consequences for following instructions, not lecturing, pleading, cajoling, or discussion.

3. When teachers feel themselves getting emotionally involved, they should:

    a. step back from situation, get it in perspective through self-talk
    b. try to put themselves in the student's position for purposes of analyzing what's happening
    c. keep channels of communication with other teachers and administrators open--initiate contact to obtain help
    d. disengage--refuse to be drawn into the argument

Managing the Discussion

One of the most difficult aspects of teaching cases is actually managing the discussion in pursuit of the questions you think are important. Planning your opening question is critical; you will need to decide whether to ask it of the group or of an individual. Sometimes it is a good idea to ask a particular student to be the first respondent to your opening question (you may privately get this person's permission to call on her or him before class) and another to provide a second response. Knowing how and when to question, how to follow up, how and when to change the course of the discussion, and so on are not easy to learn. We encourage you to read from the works we list in our references, as leading a fruitful case discussion is quite challenging.

Every group of students presents different problems when it comes to discussing cases, and we do not want to overgeneralize about how students will respond. We predict, however, that if you teach cases you will sooner or later encounter one or more of the following problems: (1) students who dominate the discussion or are extremely opinionated; (2) students who seldom or never contribute to the discussion; (3) "war stories," inappropriately personal revelations, or off-task comments.

We and others who teach cases have found it necessary to call on particular students at times to keep them in the discussion and keep others from talking too much. At times, it may be necessary to have private conversations with class members, either to encourage their participation or to help them let others participate. Requiring written answers to questions prior to beginning the case discussion will help keep the focus on relevant issues. Another strategy we have found extremely helpful is breaking the class into smaller groups in which they prepare their thoughts before sharing them with the whole class.

Arranging the Classroom for Case Teaching

Class discussions often occur in classrooms with desks arranged in rows, but these discussions tend to be limited primarily to short bursts of exchange between instructor and students. Case teaching is greatly facilitated by a classroom arrangement in which students can see each other, establish eye contact easily, and know each others' names. The best arrangement seems to be a semicircle of chairs. We prefer to have students prepare name cards and keep them on their desks so that they learn each others' names and can use their names in asking questions of or responding to each other. The semicircle arrangement also allows the instructor to move easily among the students, using proximity as an additional means of controlling the flow of discussion. It also allows the instructor to keep track of the discussion on a chalkboard or chart paper at the front of the room.

The chalkboard or chart is an important feature of most case teaching. It is not necessary to record every comment or idea as the discussion unfolds, but what you write will be helpful in keeping track of the points you think are important. Without the board or chart, you and your students run the risk of becoming confused about what has been said and where the discussion is going. What goes on the board or chart should not be an afterthought; you must think through ahead of class where you believe the discussion should go, yet be ready to modify your plan on the basis of students' responses.

Thinking Through a Board Outline

We and others have found it helpful during our preparation to try to imagine what the chalkboard or chart paper might look like as we discuss the case and record important points for the class. The case outline provides the facts of the case as you choose to organize them in your mind; the board outline shows how the discussion might unfold in response to your questions. Of course, the actual material on the board or chart paper may be considerably different from what you predict, depending on students' responses and insights (and your own as you teach the case). Still, we have found that preparing a board outline in advance helps us focus the discussion on the points we think are most important. Following is a board outline one of us prepared after formulating questions for "John McCullum." Again, keep in mind that another instructor's board outline--or the outline of the same instructor taking a different approach to the case--might look quite different. Notice also that the board outline does not address every question we thought of using. We have boxed material that we envision as a section on the board or a page of chart paper.

Board outline, "WHAT YOU DON'T KNOW CAN HURT YOU! John McCullum"

Central Problem

power struggle
obsession with control
noncompliance
lack of stimulus control
failure to find & use pos. reinf.
lack of consistency, predictability
.
.

Other Problems

lack of supervision
    poor planning
racial/ethnic tension

.
.

People

John, stud. tchr.
15 8th graders, 7th per.
  7 high-achieving (1 bl. female)
  8 low-achieving (7 bl. 1 w. male)
  Richard
  Chris
clin. inst.
sub. tchr.
asst. princ. (Mr. Roberts)
stud. in hall
Eng. tchr.

Places

John's clasrm
hallway
bike rack
office

Episodes

1.   quiz game, 7th period:
         grouping trouble
         argument, hostile exchange
         Richard runs

2.   bike rack, after sch. that day
         Richard won't talk

3.   office, next morning
         Richard makes threatening comments
         John responds angrily

4.   Richard in class, that afternoon
         supposed to have been in ISS
         low-key, calm
         refuses to stay for detention

5.   detention after school, next afternoon
         Richard didn't come to class (in ISS)
         Mr. Roberts told Richard to come to detention
         John tries to explain detention
         Richard becomes erratic

(Note: If class seems uncertain of sequence of events, perhaps develop more detail, as in case outline.)

Possible Intervention Points

Episode 1: Quiz Game

Related to planning and grouping
        stayed with clin. instructor's methods
        asked clin. instructor or other tchr. for help in planning
        hetero. ability groups (coop lrn.)
        apparent random grouping
        make sure all groups have some success ...
Related to argument
        referral of both at first argument ...
At second hostile exchange
        talk only to Chris, ignore Richard's running ...

Episode 2: Bike Rack, After School

Richard's refusal to talk
        start by finding something pos. to say
        ask nonthreatening question first
        say he'd like to talk tomorrow ...
John's indignation
        try to get incident in perspective
        consider alternatives to referral ...

Episode 3: Office, Next Morning

On way to office
        talked about other nonthreatening things as well as detention...
Copying (what but ignore?)
Water fountain
        ignore
        take immediately to Mr. Roberts
        calm, soft reprimand ...

Note: Review all 6 points from previous discussion, then choose those to explore in depth.)

Devising a Teaching Strategy

One of the special pleasures (and challenges) of teaching a case-based course is finding new ways to get oneself and one's students cognitively and affectively involved in each case. A straightforward approach to analyzing characters, events, management strategies, and outcomes through discussion guided by artful questioning is one approach--and one that we recommend you become comfortable in using before you experiment with alternatives. We have found that our students respond enthusiastically to this approach, particularly early in a semester but even after they have had experience with numerous cases.

After you have acquired skill in a more straightforward approach, however, you may want to look for ways to enliven discussion and interaction among your students. We offer brief descriptions of teaching strategies we have used successfully with several of our cases. You may want to try variations on what we have done or devise completely different strategies.

MELINDA SMITH: They failed Derrick. The instructor might play multiple roles, in this case the roles of Melinda, Greg, Derrick, Mrs. Yates, Barbara, and Joey as depicted in Part A. Students may ask any of the characters any question they like to explore the events, attitudes, feelings, and decisions of the characters. The questioning can be very revealing of what students see as important in understanding what is happening in this case before they encounter Part B. This requires the role-player's sticking to the facts of the case as presented, but exploring possible motivations and perceptions of the individuals involved. An alternative is to assign particular students to play the roles of the characters in Part A. Questioning after the students have read Part B may then explore how their perceptions of characters and events and how their thinking about appropriate management might have changed.

JANET LANE: The truth about Alice. In teaching this case, we have sometimes divided the class into three groups, representing Janet, Alice, and Mitch. Each group is to decide how their character would describe the other two, including how they would describe the others to the principal. We use this strategy to help students understand the thinking and perceptions of the various characters in this case.

REBECCA PHILLIPS: The contract with Parrish and son. This case provides an ideal opportunity to role-play talking to a student who is in obvious emotional distress. We may ask students to play the roles of Rebecca and Bob and have them try out various ways in which Rebecca might have responded to Bob at different points in the case (e.g., his first complaint about the home-school contract, the material he entered in his journal, his running out of the room). Another device we have used is having students write the home-school contract as they think it should have been written.

JANE LEE: Whose class is this?. This case provides a natural opportunity to ask students to predict what Jane wrote to Belinda or, alternatively, to write what they believe Jane should have written. We have used questioning and discussion with Part A of this case, then asked students to compose a letter (either what they think Jane wrote, knowing what they do about her, or what they think she should have written). Students then volunteer to read their letters and explain why they wrote what they did; others question or make suggestions. Finally, we present Part B, compare what Jane wrote to what students wrote, and discuss the similarities and differences.

Finding and Using Additional Cases

We believe you will find the cases included in our text sufficient for a full semester of teaching. However, you may wish to explore other sources of cases for highlighting particular problems or issues.

Written Cases

You may, of course, wish to write one or more cases of your own. In addition, you may find cases of interest in the following:

1. Shulman, J. H., & Colbert, J. A. (1988). The intern teacher casebook. Far West Laboratory for Educational Research and Development, 1855 Folsom Street, San Francisco, CA 94103.

2. Shulman, J. H., & Colbert, J. A. (1987). The mentor teacher casebook. Far West Laboratory for Educational Research and Development, 1855 Folsom Street, San Francisco, CA 94103.

Good cases on film or video tape are not easy to find, partly because case-based teaching is still relatively new to teacher training and partly because filming and taping present special problems of cost and inability to protect identities. However, we suggest that you consider the following:

1. "Jerry O'Dell: Beginning Teacher (Second Semester)." color videotape cassette, approximately 30 min. This video case was prepared specifically for teacher training and includes instructional and behavior management issues in each segment. Specific segments include greeting children at the beginning of the day, checking homework, a math board game, storytime, language arts, and a final disciplinary problem. For information, write Commonwealth Center for the Education of Teachers, University of Virginia, Ruffner Hall, 405 Emmet Street, Charlottesville, VA 22903.

2. "Videotaped Cases of Culturally Diverse Classrooms." color videotape cassettes, produced under a grant from Hitachi Corporation, of cases that highlight instructional and behavior management as well as multicultural issues. For information, write Commonwealth Center for the Education of Teachers, University of Virginia, Ruffner Hall, 405 Emmet Street, Charlottesville, VA 22903.

3. "Kids Are People, Too." 16mm color film, approximately 45 min. (two reels). A Laurence Loewinger film; Stephen Curtin, editor; produced by Macmillan Films; distributed by the Center for Urban Education, Yew York, NY. This film, made in the early 1970s, tells the story of a first-year teacher of a special class for disruptive fourth grade boys. Although dated in some respects, it presents many relevant issues for discussion, including issues related to behavior management, instruction, cultural bias, and professional relationships.

Part III. Completion of Cases (Parts B)

Following are Parts B of the cases for which a Part A is designated in the students' textbook. In our experience, Part B of a case can be used much more effectively when students do not have access to it until after they have studied Part A and recommended a course of action or predicted what is likely to happen next. After reading Part B, students may reflect on their recommendations or predictions based on Part A of the case; and they may then, with the benefit of additional information, recommend a course of action based on the entire case.

Part B

Helen's session with Cindy had helped her sort out what she believed to be true about this entire situation with Justin and his family. She concluded that there were emotional problems and possibly learning disability problems that caused Justin to experience so much difficulty in school. Helen also believed that she was not equipped to handle these problems, and that it was now time to seek the expertise of more qualified personnel. Hence, the week following the meeting with the Richardsons, Helen brought Justin's case before the child study committee and asked that they once again pursue the testing that had been recommended the previous year.

Now, a month after the committee meeting, Helen found Cindy seated before her and once again felt the need to share the details of her most recent episode with Justin. It was a Sunday afternoon, and she and Cindy had just dotted the last "i" and crossed the last "t" of their plans for the week. Plan books, schedules, blackline masters, and teachers' manuals were scattered about the floor.

"Though we may toil from sun to sun, a teacher's work is never done," quipped Cindy as she began to clean up her part of the mess.

"You're telling me!" groaned Helen. She began to pack the rectangular laundry basket that she used to transport materials to and from school. "I'm really excited about the activities I've planned for this week, but I honestly dread the thought of dealing with Justin Richardson for another day. I feel like Judy--I feel like I'm on a treadmill with this kid."

"So what's happening now?" Cindy asked. "Didn't you tell me that the child study committee made recommendations that you thought might work?"

"So I thought," agreed Helen as she placed the last stack of materials into her make-shift brief case. "I shared the experiences I've had with the Richardsons' and my conversations with Judy. After hearing my concerns, the team concluded that there was a slim-to-none chance that Mr. and Mrs. Richardson would reconsider having Justin evaluated. Instead, they recommended that we try Judy's strategy. They suggested that Ron Saunders--that itinerant school psychologist assigned to our building--work with me as a consultant. I wasn't exactly thrilled about that decision, but I understood, to some degree anyway, why they didn't want to pursue testing or counseling, and I felt that with help from a more experienced professional I might be able to help Justin."

"Well?" Cindy asked.

Well, I was <u>dead</u> wrong!" replied Helen. "This child is determined to have his way, and he lets me and everyone else at the school know that he simply will not be broken. He is so defiant in a nagging, passive sort of way, and he isn't bothered in the least bit by any of the consequences that we built into his contract. I really want to help this kid, but I'm losing patience. I'm beginning to resent having to meet and plan so much for some kid who just doesn't respond positively to anything."

"OK, OK!" Cindy interjected, motioning Helen to calm down. "What exactly did the two of you come up with?"

"We worked like gangbusters! After the child study team made its recommendations, Ron and I met several times to discuss Justin's case and brainstorm about possible behavior management strategies. Finally, we decided that self-recording of completed assignments might motivate him to finish more of his work. We developed daily recording sheets and set up a plan to monitor his performance. We had a little meeting with Justin and developed a menu of rewards that would encourage him to complete at least 50 percent of his math assignments per week. We also wrote up a weekly contract that outlined expectations and consequences."

"Well, are you ready for this? The self-recording thing didn't even last a week. Justin rushed through all of his math assignments without reading or copying the problems from his textbook. He simply headed his paper, filled in the blank spaces with numbers that he apparently pulled from the sky, and placed his papers in the 'assignments completed' box. His work completion rate skyrocketed, but his accuracy rate plummeted."

Cindy could understand Helen's frustration, but she could not help chuckling when she realized that Justin had manipulated the situation one more time. "So the infamous Justin prevails again," she noted.

"You guessed it. And at that point I was seeing red. My teeth ached, I was so tensed up. I just felt like grabbing Justin by his shoulders and shaking some sense into him."

"Helen, I know exactly how you feel. It's really difficult to deal with a kid that you just can't seem to reach, even though you've given it your best shot. Try not to take this thing so personally, and remember that Justin's learned to play his games well. It may take a long time to eliminate his inappropriate behaviors."

"I know, I know," continued Helen. "We didn't give up so easily. Ron and I both agreed that we were pretty stupid not to include anything about accuracy in Justin's contract, so we added in a statement that he would also have to complete his math assignments with at least 50 percent accuracy."

"Sounds good," Cindy stated, "but I take it from the look on your face that this didn't work either."

"Right again," replied Helen. "To get around this added contingency, our little friend proceeded to cheat from his neighbors' papers. This time, both work completion and accuracy increased, and of course Justin claimed that he was meeting the terms of the contract. Friday, after carefully observing and documenting Justin's behavior for three days, I decided that I had to confront him. That's when things really got out of hand."

"While everyone else completed their independent practice assignments for math, I called Justin to my desk, reviewed the terms of the contract, and questioned him about the cheating.

" 'I didn't cheat off of nobody's paper, you liar!' This is exactly what he screamed at me! The other kids stopped working and looked up to see what was going on. Then Justin really went into his act. He grabbed the contract off my desk, ripped it up, ran into the bathroom in the back of the classroom, and slammed the door behind him. I was totally caught off guard because I'd never seen him act this way before."

"Yeah, sometimes that happens when you implement a management program," said Cindy. "As you tighten the reigns, the kid resists. So how in the world did you pull things together after that outburst?"

"Believe me, it wasn't easy. I walked to the bathroom door and asked Justin to come out. No response. I opened the door, and I immediately dismissed any thought of trying to force him out. I mean, he looked crazed! He had his fists clinched, his eyes were bulging, and his whole body was shaking. Hey, I politely closed the door. 'No way,' I thought, 'not today.'"

"I turned around and looked at the other kids. Some of them asked, 'What's wrong with Justin, Miss Jamison?' Others started laughing, and within seconds they were all chattering about what had just happened. I stood in the middle of the classroom, not knowing what to say or do."

"Finally, I remembered Ron's crisis intervention plan, so I sent a student to his office with an SOS card. Ron got there in a few minutes, and while he attended to Justin I took the rest of the class outside for an unplanned recess period. That seemed to take their minds off of what had just happened."

"Well, young lady, I think you did a super job of handling things," replied Cindy.

"Yeah, I was really glad that I was able to get the other kids out of the room without creating another major scene. After about 30 minutes, Ron convinced Justin to come out of the bathroom, and he took him to his office for the rest of the day.
"And what's the plan for tomorrow?" asked Cindy.

"Well, Ron and I talked to our principal after school and he has put us on the agenda to meet with the child study committee first thing tomorrow morning. I don't know what the final outcome will be, but I do know that something has to change. Justin has some serious emotional problems, and I think it's pretty obvious that, right now, he needs more than I'm able to give."

Part B

When I reached Derrick's seat at the table, I kneeled so that our eyes met at the same level. I spoke in a calm voice. "Derrick, I understand that you had a knife on the bus. Is this true?"

"Yeah, I have a knife. So, what of it?" he replied mockingly.

I asked him to give me the knife, and that's when he really lost it for the first time in my classroom. His shout was so loud that I know people at the other end of the hall heard him.

"Who told you, anyway? I'm going to get the bastard who told on me. This is my knife, I bought it with my own money and you ain't getting it--I don't care what you say, you ain't getting it!"

Oh, Lord have mercy! I thought. Here we go. He walked to his seat and started laughing uncontrollably. He had the knife in his hand, but he hadn't opened it. I was more than a little nervous at this point, and I feared that things might really get out of hand. I knew that I had to react in a way that would not reveal my fears, and at the same time I didn't want to do anything that would cause Derrick to react physically. He continued to look at me. The smile on his face showed all of his bucked, crooked teeth, just as Barbara had told me at the beginning of the year. And yes, he <u>did</u> look like something very, very scary.

I continued to talk with him and told him calmly that carrying weapons on school property, including the school bus, was not permissible, that I could not let him keep it, and that he would need to calm down. I used a crisis intervention strategy that I learned as a special educator. As I talked with him, whenever I saw anything that resembled calmness, I offered social reinforcement.

"Good, Derrick. You're not screaming now. You're talking in a calm voice, and you're very still. Good job, now let me have the knife."

Finally, to my relief, he extended his hand with the knife and said, "Here, you want the knife, take it. Give it to the principal if you want to."

"Thank you. What a good idea!" I responded. "Normally when I take something from a student, I let it stay on my desk, and then I send it home with a note to the parents. In this case, though, because this is a weapon, I think you're absolutely right. Taking it to Mr. Rodgers is a great idea!"

So we both took the knife to the office, and I explained that we were not coming with just bad news. I told Greg about the knife, but I also explained that Derrick had suggested that we bring the knife to the office. Because Greg and I went back a long way, we were able to make use of some of the signals that we used in the old days. I managed to catch his eye when Derrick wasn't looking, and a quick wink from me let him know that everything was under control. Greg told Derrick that he didn't want this to happen again and that he would keep the knife until Mrs. Yates could come to school and pick it up. Greg also warned that the next time more serious action would be taken.

I was relieved. I thought we had managed to resolve this conflict and defuse any explosion that might have occurred. Derrick was calm now, and I suspected that things would go rather smoothly for the rest of the day. So much for wishful thinking. Derrick decided to extend his little morning drama into a mini-series. He left the room three or four times that afternoon. He didn't use the bathroom pass, he simply got up and left the room and stayed out 15 to 20 minutes each time. I suddenly realized that these first few weeks of school had been merely the calm before the storm.

Derrick was truly trying to test me. He knew that I had a policy in my room. He knew that, in a very short time, I had established a relationship of trust within the classroom. I allowed my students--very responsible students--to go to the restroom without asking permission. All they had to do was get up from their seats quietly, take one of the wooden bathroom passes, and leave with the understanding that they were not to abuse the privilege. Even though the rule wasn't etched in stone, they were to be back within five minutes and were not to leave the room more than once within any given hour. I explained to them all the time that this was an honor, that they were the oldest students in the building, and that I expected them to handle this privilege. I said to them all the time, "If you abuse, you lose." So Derrick took it upon himself to challenge me on this rule.

The last time he got up and left the room, he stayed for about 20 minutes. He reentered and walked over to my desk. We had just finished math, and the other students were preparing for their reading lesson. I was gathering the materials that were needed for the lesson, and I tried my best not to show that I was upset with him. He looked at me and smiled.

"I've been out a long time," he mumbled.

I picked up my materials and faced him with a look of concern and answered, "Yes, I noticed you were out. Is everything OK?"

"Yeah, I thought we couldn't stay that long."

I had to use every ounce of restraint that I possessed as I thought about my next response. I knew that any expression of outrage on my part would send him into hysterics and he'd probably wreck the classroom. No, that wouldn't work. It had never worked before. I had to second guess this child. I had to hit him from an unexpected angle and catch him off guard. So, once again, I decided to down play the entire episode.

"Well you're right. You were out for quite a while--but you know what, I trust you. I thought you needed to be out."

"Naw, sometimes I had to use the bathroom, but sometimes I was just walking around in the halls. One time, I even went outside and walked around."

"Keep your cool," I thought. "Remember, you have to figure out a way to make the whole thing--Derrick's game plan--backfire." I decided to use the old "honesty is the best policy" routine once more.

"Well, Derrick, I must thank you again for being up front with me. I really appreciate that you have been honest about what you did. You know, some students would not be truthful in the way that you have been. Now, I want you to understand that if this happens again, you are going

36

to lose the privilege of going out of the class to use the bathroom or a drink of water without permission. I hope you understand this."

Not giving him the opportunity to respond, I made a shushing gesture with my hand and told him to prepare for the next lesson. After I spoke, Derrick stared at me with a puzzled look on his face. "Ah-hah! My little strategy is working," I thought. He didn't know what to think of me. He anticipated that I would start yelling and screaming at him and send him to the office--just as all his other teachers had done. When I chose something positive about the situation, he did not know what to think or say. He just stared at me for an instant without the air of confidence and control that I had observed earlier. Once more, I was hopeful. Maybe this approach would work.

For the next month, things did go rather smoothly. Oh, there were several times when Derrick decided to show off or create a disturbance, but I continued to remain calm throughout. I was trying hard to let him know that I was not going to give in to his desire to make me "lose it" in the classroom. For a month, though he had his little outbursts, he never won. Occasionally, he beat on his desk with a pencil, rattled papers, made animal noises, and burped loudly, but these episodes started to occur less and less frequently. Once again, proximity control and signaling were all that it took to get him back on track.

The fact that my other students were just the best kids that any teacher could ever hope to have also helped the situation. Whenever Derrick was absent or out of the room, I would talk to them about ignoring inappropriate behaviors. We would even practice how to respond when he left the room and reentered after a long period of time or reentered after I had had to take him outside of the classroom for what I called a teacher-student interaction.

Things were going great, and just when I thought we were out of the woods, Derrick decided to try a new tactic. I came to the conclusion that he could not be satisfied if we were functioning in a state of equilibrium. The child liked excitement and adventure in his life. So, since he couldn't coerce me into a standoff in the classroom, he started to terrorize the other students.

Once, he decided to get his kicks by ripping up his classmates' spelling papers. Literally, before I could get to him, he got up and proceeded to rip the papers of all the students in his row. The poor kids didn't say a word. They were angry and frightened. As quickly as I could, I got over to Derrick and told him to stop--that his behavior was inappropriate. He looked directly at me and laughed, but he stopped tearing the papers. Then I asked him to step outside so that we could have our little interaction. By now the others knew that when I had to do this, they were to continue working quietly. Anyway, I had to do this because I didn't want to embarrass this kid or set him off in front of the other students. So, we stepped outside the door of my classroom and talked. As usual, I talked to him about his inappropriate behavior and described to him what he should have been doing. Then I described his punishment. He would have to apologize to the students and stay after school to tape the ripped papers back together. It worked pretty well.

When we reentered the classroom, the other students didn't say a word. They didn't even look up, but continued to concentrate on their work until I announced that Derrick had something to say. They accepted his apology and went right back to their assignments, just the way we had practiced. What a wonderful class! They were with me all the way on this one. In times to come, I realized that I couldn't have handled Derrick without them. They were truly a great bunch!

Sometimes during our discussions when Derrick was out of the room, they would ask me what they were supposed to do when he took one of their pencils and broke it or what to do if he ever hit one of them. I told them that I watched Derrick as closely as possible and that I would continue to intervene when I saw him do something inappropriate. If he did something that I was unaware of, I told them to get to me and let me know. We continued to practice ignoring skills when he decided to have his uncontrollable hiccups or burping spells. I explained that Derrick had gotten the attention of everyone else by doing things that were not acceptable to others. If we could ignore those behaviors and try to look at the good things that he did and tell him about it, then maybe he would change.

Because Derrick never hit one of the students, their fear of him began to wane and eventually, if he worked well in a cooperative learning group, or if I made a big deal out of some good work that he'd completed, they praised him just as they praised anyone else in the class.

Finally, Derrick started to take to this special treatment. By Christmas, the frequency of his outbursts in the classroom had decreased drastically. The students were more comfortable with him, and they really wanted to see him make it in our class. Things were much better within the confines of our classroom, but . . . well,. . . outside the classroom Derrick continued to seek ways to satisfy his insatiable need for calamity. Still, I felt that his improved behavior in the classroom was a giant step in the right direction.

It was just about time for Christmas break, and I was really feeling good about Derrick. I thought we might end the first half of the year on a pleasant note, but Derrick decided otherwise. One day I saw him get up quietly, get the bathroom pass, and leave the room to go to the bathroom. From the corner of my eye, I could see that he had been working nicely, and he appeared to be working at a steady pace. I was simply thrilled! Even his academic work had improved a great deal. It just so happened that on this day there was an overflow in the first floor boy's bathroom, and the custodian blocked the doorway so that he could clean up the mess. Apparently, Derrick decided to proceed to the second floor bathroom. The rest of the story is a nightmare. I looked at the clock and realized that Derrick had been out of the room for about 15 minutes.

"That's strange," I thought, "He hasn't done this in weeks." I started to get a little worried, so I sent another student, Andre, to the restroom to find him. In a few minutes, Andre rushed in to tell me that Derrick was upstairs and was holding up Mr. Douglas, the assistant principal, in the bathroom. Later, Mr. Douglas related that he had seen Derrick wandering around upstairs, so he had asked him what he was doing there. He reported that Derrick walked up to him with a crazed look in his eyes and shouted at him repeatedly, "Do you want to die today, huh?" Mr. Douglas was frightened at this point, and he ran into the bathroom and closed the door. After hearing calls for help, one of the fourth grade teachers sent for Greg, and he arrived upstairs with the custodian within minutes. The three men physically took Derrick to the office. This was two days before Christmas break. Derrick was suspended from school until after the holidays.

When we returned to school in January, the placement team went into high gear to get Derrick evaluated for special education. Near the end of January, Derrick was identified as having a behavioral disorder, and the team recommended--because of his size and because we did not have such a class in our school--that Derrick be sent to the nearby middle school. This really bothered me. All things considered, I thought we were doing pretty well. In spite of acting out, leaving the room, and the incident with the assistant principal, we'd had no major catastrophes. Nothing happened that I hadn't been able to handle within the classroom singlehandedly. I thought that Derrick was on the road to existing in a classroom without feeling he had to be in total control of the teacher and the other students. I tried to convince Greg and the team to give us more time, but there was no way that I could change their minds.

And so Derrick's mother brought him to get his things, and I gave him a pad and pencil set as a going away present. I told him that the kids and I would miss him and that the class wouldn't be the same without him. He began to sob uncontrollably, and he just kept telling me over and over again that he didn't want to leave. All I could do was hold him until his mother pulled him away and led him out of the classroom. I couldn't move. I was drained. I was devastated. We had worked so hard and we were making progress. Now, it seemed that all of our efforts had been in vain.

We failed Derrick Yates. He went to the middle school program and within two weeks was expelled for cursing his teacher. Shortly after that, he was admitted to the local mental hospital, where he's been for the last month.

Part B

It occurred to Paul that he may have no choice other than to risk hurting the substitute's feelings. The break had to be made. In order to make it as quietly as possible, he managed to signal Irene to the side. "Would you mind telling Cathy that I would like to get started," he hinted. Irene was quick to grasp his meaning, and she immediately pulled Cathy aside and earnestly whispered the message in her ear.

Cathy's smile vanished from her face and was replaced with a sad but comprehending expression. She approached him resolutely. "Sorry to be hanging around. I know you've got to get on with this. Would it be okay if I come back to visit sometimes, though? I got pretty attached to these kids while I was here."

"Sure," Paul assented. "I think that'd be good for them. They could use the sense of continuity, from what I understand."

Cathy's eyes brightened with interest, and she began offering him her perspective on how the situation should be handled. "I tried not to be too strict on them because I think they've had enough of that. As long as they did their work, I let them listen to their Walkmans at their desks. We took breaks in the morning for snacks and games. These kids have been through a lot."

Paul purposely avoided offering any evaluation of her methods, not indicating how he planned to proceed. It would be pointless and would only create discomfort. He simply listened quietly, and she interpreted his silence as unanimity. He punctuated her litany by reiterating with feigned enthusiasm, "Sure. Come back and visit. It'd be great."

Cathy correctly interpreted this vague invitation as a cue to depart. "Okay, well...good luck. Let me know if I can do anything," she offered on her way out the door.

Paul gave her a friendly smile, nodding affirmatively. "Thanks, I will," he assured her. He turned toward the class.

In the back of the classroom, the nine boys and one girl were busy with the new games. Irene moved from one group to the next, admonishing them to put the games away, but her directives were met with benign disregard. Paul repeated the request to put the games away as he walked toward them. Suddenly, all eyes were on him. An awkward silence hung in the air. "Ms. Walker, please help them get those games put away," Paul requested politely but matter-of-factly. As she began to pick up game pieces, the students slowly pitched in to help. Paul gave a shallow sigh of relief that this situation had not turned into a confrontation. But he knew it was coming. It had to be coming.

After completing the milk money collection and taking attendance, he briefly introduced himself. In doing so, he intentionally avoided any commentary about the past or the future. He did not want to deliver a "This-is-how-it's-going-to-be-from-now-on-around-here" pronouncement or make any other sweeping remarks that might be interpreted as his "throwing down the gauntlet." They would get to know him over time, he thought.

40

More important, he needed time to get to know them before he could make sound judgements about how to pull this class back together.

The first order of business was to get Irene to lead the class in a learning activity that he had planned: classifying animals. He had deliberately made the lesson easy for her to lead and interesting for the students. It was structured in such a way that he could pull students individually from the group for informal assessment without significantly disrupting their participation. This was his first step in actually getting a handle on their learning needs.

He was aware that his assessment might be disconcerting to the students, so he explained to each one at the beginning of his 15 minutes that he was not grading them but just trying to get some information about the best way to teach them. He did his best to convey sincerity and a sense of quiet confidence.

These kids need to feel secure around me, he thought. But I can't give away my authority all the way either. It's going to take a careful balance.

Each student cooperated tentatively while Paul administered fluency and comprehension probes. By the end of the morning, he felt that he had gathered valuable information and had made some initial inroads toward developing a rapport with his students.

At lunch, Paul made it a point to watch his students' social interactions. He noticed during the course of the meal that Shane had gathered all of the boys at the very end of the long lunch table. He wore an acrimonious expression as he delivered a monologue, to which the others attended in apparent fascination. Paul didn't know what to make of it, but an intuitive alarm went off in his subconscious. Fortunately, lunch was about over, so he called the students together to go to the restroom and return to the classroom.

During the afternoon, Paul had planned a social studies lesson on reading maps. He began by telling the students about the maps were used by explorers long ago. He described the Vikings and others who had explored North America and about Christopher Columbus, who was subsequently credited with the discovery of America. As he instructed the class as a whole group, it occurred to him that he had their full attention, which pleased him. The only problem was that they interrupted him and each other so frequently that what began as an interesting lesson deteriorated into a veritable tower of babble. Paul repeatedly reminded them to raise their hands and wait to be called upon, but to no avail. He realized that they were not intentionally being noncompliant but had, in Jane Abbott's words, "some bad habits." They were, after all, interrupting him and each other with comments and questions relevant to the topic. I'll have to get a handle on this right away, Paul thought as he worked to keep the class on track. He had a strong hunch that he could address many of the behavioral problems by delivering a strong and interesting instructional program to these students. So, the first order of business was to work on the behaviors requisite to keep interesting lessons on track.

After school, Paul and Irene went about straightening the room and performing organizational chores. "There's something I think you should know," Irene ventured.

"What?" Paul asked, half dreading the news.

41

"You know, at lunch when Shane had all of the boys down at the end of the lunch table? They were planning a revolt. Cynthia told me about it. She said that most of them didn't really want to do it, but Shane is sort of a leader," Irene went on.

"Well, I don't know what to say," Paul replied. "I suppose they want to test the limits. They're probably still confused about what happened the first semester. I'm not going to worry about it," he concluded. He sat down at his desk to complete some paper work as Irene retrieved her coat and purse.

"Have a good afternoon," she offered cheerfully as she headed for the door.

"You do the same," Paul responded absently.

The following morning, his 10 students filed into the classroom quietly. Each cast him a surreptitious glance, put away their coats, and gathered at the back of the classroom to play with the boxed games. Oops, Paul thought. I forgot about dealing with that situation. But as he watched them organize the games and choose partners, it occurred to him that it might be a good idea to let this ritual stand. Playing these games might be a good forum for developing social skills; and, although he could think of better uses of this time while students were arriving and he was completing the morning accounting, rocking the boat too hard too soon could be a mistake. He walked back to watch, standing far enough away that the students would not feel that he was invading their space. In the few minutes he watched them, he noticed that Shane seemed to be the one the other students esteemed. He was a wiry 12-year-old who played with an intensity and purpose that the others seemed to lack. Soon, everyone was engrossed in watching him beat Ricky in a game of Connect Four.

At the conclusion of the game, Paul told Shane and Ricky they could continue to play until all of the students arrived and he had collected milk money and taken roll, but they would have to be at their seats and ready for work at 8:45 sharp. They seemed to accept his edict.

Later that morning, Paul left Irene in charge of the class while he went to the restroom. As he returned, he could hear angry voices from the room.

"You little issue," he heard Vincent bellow.

"Nigger!" Brian shot back.

Whoa, Paul thought. Rounding the door frame, he made his presence seem larger than life by putting on a quiet, stern demeanor. All fell silent, and the students went back to their work.

Paul approached Irene at the back table. She was staring pink-faced down at the table. "What happened?" he whispered.

"Vincent got mad at Brian because he wouldn't loan him some paper. You came back just about that time. I'm glad you did. That Vincent, he's a big fella. Brian could've gotten himself creamed," she explained.

"What is an 'issue?'" Paul asked incredulously.

Irene whispered, "It's what people around here call kids who are part Native American and part black. Really, Brian is both, plus his mother is white."

"It's not a nice word," she added.

"I gathered that," Paul replied. He let it drop at that, partly because he felt uncertain about what to say to Vincent and Brian. To hear them be so cruel to each other left him with a vague, sick-hearted feeling. He also surmised that it was not safe to leave Irene in the classroom alone. He almost asked her why she had not intervened, but he did not want to sound accusatory or disapproving. It was clear that the students did not view her as an adult authority, and this would be a handicap.

At the beginning of social studies, Paul began his solution for the interruptions:

You know, yesterday we were so interested in talking about the Vikings and other explorers that we got off track because we were all trying to talk at once. I was glad that you wanted to ask questions and offer comments, but it's awfully hard to hear each other when too much talking is going on. Because it's easy to forget to raise our hands when we really get excited about the subject, I have an idea to help us. I'm giving each of you an index card to put on your desk. There's a block for each subject period. Here's what we're going to do. If you slip up and talk without being called on, put a mark like this [he demonstrated a check mark] on the block of the subject we are working in. Let's see how low we can keep these marks. For now, let's try to keep the marks down to two or less.

The students seemed to like the idea, and when they had gotten their self-monitoring cards situated on their desks, Paul continued with the unit on maps. He reviewed yesterday's discussion, and most of the students managed to abide by the hand-raising rule. Ricky was the first to interrupt, and immediately the others jeered him. Paul intervened immediately. "No, don't do that," Paul persuaded them. "All of us will make a slip-up sometimes. Ricky knew he forgot as soon as he did it, so we don't need to make a big deal of it. Let's let each person take care of himself." Several students nodded in agreement, and Paul proceeded with the lesson.

As he introduced the lines of latitude and longitude, he drew a model of the globe and the lines on the board. He had never been very good at drawing, and the earth looked a bit lopsided. He talked, as he drew, about how latitude and longitude help us locate places on a map.

Suddenly, Shane proclaimed, "You're not doing it right."

Paul looked up a bit startled. "What's wrong?" he asked.

"You don't have enough lines. It doesn't look like the one in the book here," Shane stated derisively. With a thinly veiled smirk of superiority he added, "You don't know what you're doing. You can't teach."

It was true that his model was not very good. "Okay," Paul stated. Let's just all look at the model in the book. Tell us what page it's on, Shane."

Shane slammed the book shut. "You're supposed to know," he challenged.

Paul quickly picked up his book, found the illustration, and announced the page number. By now he was really feeling off balance. The rest of the class clearly was enjoying the spectacle. Shane wore a smug smile, and the other students were snickering surreptitiously. A slow flame of anger began rising in Paul. Something was happening here that he could not quite get a handle on; yet, he sensed somehow it was critical that he do so.

Part B

As Robert examined the watch, he confronted David indirectly by asking him in a disbelieving tone of voice if he realized what a strange coincidence it was that Bob's lost watch and the one David claimed his father gave him were the same watch. David immediately refuted him, saying, "No it's not. My dad gave me this one. No it's not! No it's not!"

At this point, Robert decided to take David to the principal's office, where he presented the situation to her and David's special education teacher. David's learning disabilities resource teacher, Lisa Griffith, added that she had noticed David was wearing the watch when he came back to her classroom before getting ready to go home the previous day. Still, David insisted that his father had given it to him. Incredulous and frustrated, Robert at last told David that they would just have to telephone his father to verify his story. Surely, he thought, he'll break down and tell the truth now. Offering him one final opportunity to come clean, Robert asked, "Now, are you sure your father gave you the watch? To his utter amazement, David replied, "Yes, you call him up and that's what he's going to say."

Aware that he now had no choice but to phone his father, Robert proceeded to do so. The task was complicated by the fact that David's father worked out of town and had a hearing impairment, making it necessary for someone to serve as an interpreter on the father's end. For these reasons, Robert decided to call David's mother first. After Robert had explained the situation carefully, his mother said that David had come home with the watch and claimed that a friend, a classmate, had let him wear it. Robert thanked his mother and promised to keep her informed.

When Robert presented this new and contradictory information to David, he persisted with his original account. This time, Mrs. Griffith appealed to David. "We're getting pretty thick in all of this, David. Are you sure you don't want to go ahead and tell us what happened now, before we have to call your father and get him off of his job and also have someone interpret over the telephone?" To everyone's relief, David confessed that he had taken Bob's the watch.

Leaving the situation in the principal's hands, Robert and Lisa returned to their classes. When David returned several minutes later, Robert took him out into the hallway and asked him why he had not admitted in the first place that he had taken the watch. David only shrugged his shoulders and evaded eye contact. Robert pursued his questioning, "Well, don't you think there's something you need to say to Bob?" "Yeah," David replied in a weary voice.

When Robert leaned into the classroom and asked Bob to come out into the hallway, several of the students exchanged knowing glances. Bob approached them slowly and eyed David suspiciously. "I'm sorry," David blurted. Turning to Bob, Robert queried, "Bob, is there anything you want to say to David?" Turning to leave, Bob retorted, "I don't even want to talk to him."

As it turned out, the principal did not punish David in any way for his theft of the watch. Robert was surprised that the matter was simply dropped. Following the incident with the watch, however, other students' belongings disappeared. Each time a student reported a missing item, the others whispered among themselves and looked at David. Robert knew that they suspected him.

"Well," Robert thought to himself, "I don't know what it's going to take for David to redeem himself before me and the other students." At this point, he felt hurt and angry with David. It troubled him that he was never happy to see David enter the classroom in the morning, and he felt guilty that David was probably aware of his displeasure. He could not seem to dispel his disappointment that David had never really given him a chance to be his real teacher.

Part B

Dear Mrs. Dean,

I have considered your suggestion about the treats and rewards, and I do appreciate your concern. However, I don't feel it is appropriate to give treats out randomly, because it may reward whatever behavior is happening at that time. As far as small gifts go, I prefer to use earned privileges as a way of managing the children. I will be happy to use anything you send for prizes in the reading auction.

You should construe the remarks in this letter as signs of my willingness to explain my procedures as well as the theory that underlies them, not to negotiate them. I've been hired by the county and been found fit to teach this class. I intend to continue to teach in ways that I am convinced are professionally apt.

Sincerely,
Jane Lee

Jane heaved a sigh of relief once the letter was on its way. The matter was closed; a burden had been lifted from her shoulders. She had dealt firmly and professionally with Belinda Dean and had exercised her judgement to good effect. She sensed her renewed enthusiasm for dealing with the children instead of spending so much effort on the politics of parents. Her joy was short lived.

The next day, quite unexpectedly, Art Dean arrived to observe the fourth grade activities. Jane was uneasy. Most school board members observed classes throughout the school, looking in on different grades. Art was only interested in seeing what happened in his daughter's grade. He stayed through the PE class, playing dodge ball with Ann and observing the math class activities. Jane couldn't shake her nervousness.

Spring didn't seem pleasant any more, and Jane's heart was heavy as she tried to anticipate what was to come. She was certain that there was more to come. The unopened pack of colored pencils on her desk seemed to mock her very existence as a teacher, daring her to hand them out to her class.

Part B

Upon returning to the classroom, Jeannette settled the students into a practice activity with their weekly spelling words and asked Pat to step outside of the classroom door with her. Barely concealing her ire, she asked Pat directly what she and Judy were discussing. Pat answered frankly that they were talking about her having made Carrie sit at the lunch table by herself. Pat's candid admission disarmed her. Jeannette found herself wondering if they simply did not realize how rude and offensive they had been. She told Pat that, from now on, she wanted other teachers to come directly to her if they had a problem with her decisions. She explicitly directed Pat to, "Tell them to come to me first if they approach you with a concern." Pat agreed to do so, revealing little emotion about the incident or Jeannette's new decree.

In the course of conversations with Pat over the next several days, Jeannette began to tally the number of times Cynthia Hudson's name came up. Pat recounted any number of telephone conversations she'd recently had with Cynthia. Following one of Pat's reports about a phone conversation, Jeannette, in a strange moment of epiphany, realized how much Cynthia continued to exert influence inside and outside her classroom through Pat. Jeannette now understood that Cynthia and Pat had held continuing discussions about her classroom procedures, and that when Cynthia disapproved of Jeannette's decisions, Pat tried to "right the wrong" by assuming vicarious control of the classroom. At about the time of this revelation, Pat told Jeannette that Cynthia would soon be returning to Clearview to complete a practicum as part of her masters program. Jeannette found herself wondering anxiously, "How am I going to deal with this woman when she's actually here?"

48

Part B

1/2

A nice day! The kids--all of them including Winnie--were well behaved and cooperative. They all shared their Christmas vacations with me, and later during the day I had each of them go to the story telling station and record what they had done over the holidays. I'm going to do a whole-language thing with their stories for the next few weeks. I really like this approach. I'm still using the basal and doing some phonics, too. The use of many approaches with these kids seems to be the best way to teach them. Winnie was really calm today. He did a great job with his chart, and at the end of the day I let him go down to one of the kindergarten classes and read a story. He really enjoyed that. I hope he stays this way for a while. To say the least, such a change would be extremely therapeutic for me.

1/9

Since the last time I wrote, despite all of my positive reinforcement, Winnie has slipped back into his old ways. He's still raising his hand, but if I don't call on him right away, he continues to get upset and he acts out. He's now getting in trouble with the physical education teacher and the music teacher. He just doesn't click with either of them. Every time I go to pick up the class from music, I find Winnie in time-out because he blows up at the teacher if the instrument he wants to play is given to someone else. The same thing happens in P.E. because he can't seem to follow directions. Both teachers, though, say that Winnie's biggest problem is his mouth. They say that he just talks out. He just comes up with something out of the blue and will totally disrupt any activity to "share" whatever he's thinking. The little scenario he describes might have occurred three weeks ago, but he just has to get it out--he just has to tell you. Now Journal, I ask you, does this sound familiar, or what? I must admit that I'm somewhat relieved. I was beginning to think it was me.

2/16

The other kids really tickled me today. I'm so glad that they haven't picked up on Winnie's behavior and started to imitate him. In fact, they have started to imitate me when I praise Winnie or try to stop an outburst before it occurs. When I see him about to lose it, I have a habit of going over to him and saying, "Be strong, Winnie, be strong. I know you can do it. Just be strong."

Today, I noticed that the kids around Winnie can also see when he is about to lose it. When I was passing out paper today, Jeremy, who sits right next to Winnie, said to me, "Mrs. Gray, Winnie is doing good, today." Later, when he was getting restless and tapping his pencil on the desk, I heard a group of them saying, "Winnie, don't pout, don't pout, you can do it, be strong." How perceptive! They can predict when he's about to start his little episodes and they try to intervene. Surprisingly, sometimes it works. In this particular instance, I didn't have to say a word to him, and he stopped the tapping.

2/27

Winnie is still doing great academically, but we just can't seem to get his impulsivity under control. Today, I was giving directions to the class and he just interrupted me to tell me about a TV show he had watched last night. I walked over to his desk and gave him a check minus mark and explained to him why. Before I could get back to the front of the class, he was calling my name again. This time, I wrote his name on the board and put a check by it. He continued to talk. Nothing phases him.

3/5

Today, my central office supervisor came to observe me. This was my last observation for the year and I was really nervous. I told the kids that I'd buy a popsicle for everyone who was good and didn't get their name on the board during what I called "my test." Wouldn't you know it--Winnie was the only student who got his name on the board. He spoke out whenever he felt the urge. I was so embarrassed. I must have turned three shades of red. I tried my usual ignoring trick, and that didn't work. I tried going over to him and talking to him quietly, and that didn't work. I wrote his name on the board, and that didn't work. Finally, I threatened to take a minute from his recess every time I had to write his name on the board. With this threat, he finally settled down and I was able to continue with my lesson without further interruptions.

Fortunately, my supervisor was aware of Winnie's problems, and because all the other kids were OK, and because I had performed satisfactorily during my other observations, I passed the assessment. Still, after this incident I realized that Winnie is really draining me. He makes me feel anxious. He makes me feel like I want to scream! I want to look at him and say, "Don't talk, don't open your mouth, JUST DO NOT TALK".

Anyway, after the observer left, I just lost it with Winnie. I took him out in the hallway and decided that I would just try to reason with him. Yes, maybe if I tried to reason with him he'd realize how inappropriate his behavior really was and try to make a change. So I went up to him and said, "Winnie, do you realize what you are doing? Do you realize that you are driving me and everybody around you crazy?"

Surprisingly enough, he said, "Yeah."

I continued. "You're tapping your pencil or raising your hand, you're screaming out, you're pouting, you're walking off, you're putting your head down, and people aren't going to like you and accept you for that."

Boy, I really let him have it! He said he understood and that he would try to do better. We returned to the classroom and Winnie went straight to his seat looking really sad. I think he's truly sorry when he behaves this way, but I'm convinced that he can't really control his behavior. He wants to be good, but for some reason, he simply has to say what's on his mind whenever it's there. Anyway, he was pretty solemn for the rest of the day and my other students realized this. They felt sorry for him, and several of them walked by, patted him on the shoulder, and said, "Be strong". This really made me feel like a rat. Out of sheer frustration I had really jumped all over Winnie, and I was really sorry. Still, I think he needed to know that I was upset with him, that his behavior was really getting on my last nerve.

50

3/6

I met with Jackie again today. She's been so GREAT! My very own private support system. Anyway, I told her what happened during and after my observation. I also told her about how the threat of losing recess time had worked in getting Winnie to settle down. We decided to start from scratch. We drew up a contract stating that we wanted to cut down the amount of call outs Winnie had during the course of a day. We started with 10 being the maximum number and then we decided that after 10, I'd write his name on the board. For every call out after 10, I'd place a check mark signifying that he'd lost a minute's worth of recess time. We figured that this would really kill him because all of the other boys would be outside ripping and running, and he'd have to sit and watch. More important, if he was able to limit the number of call outs to 10 or fewer, he'd earn tokens that could be traded for prizes from Jackie's store.

3/7

We met with Winnie and I explained to him that I was losing a minute from teaching every time I had to stop what I was doing, go over to the board where his name was written, make a check mark, and return to what I was doing. Because I had to do this, he would owe me a minute when he couldn't control himself--when he called out without permission more than 10 times during the day. Winnie understood the terms of the contract. I wrote a long note to his mother explaining what we were going to do and I indicated that I would place the contract and the chart on his desk on Monday and I would send it home on Friday for her to sign and return.

3/30

We've been implementing our new plan for almost three weeks now with only marginal success. Winnie has not once gotten 10 or fewer call outs in a day despite the fact that I always prompt him. I'll say, "Winnie, you're doing so good! It's 12:00 and we're going to go out at 1:30 and you haven't lost any minutes yet." Or he can get to the end of the day with only a few check marks on his contract and I'll say, "If you hold on for a few more hours, you'll have a treat to take home." This makes him happy and he tries really hard, but he hasn't reached his weekly goal for one of the three weeks that we've tried this new approach. He doesn't seem to have the ability to hold out for that long term goal. Sometimes I think that something comes over him and he just snaps--his mind just snaps and he's like a different person. He'll try so hard, and then all of a sudden he'll lose it. He'll start with the call outs or the pouting and lose everything he's worked for. Today, things got so bad with him that I had to send him to another first grade teacher during math just to get a break for myself. For once, I felt I needed to get through an entire lesson without any major interruptions.

4/5

Bless her heart, Jackie is still trying to help me to improve Winnie's behavior. We have continued to plan, and today, she showed my class a filmstrip about pouting. The characters in the strip talked about how pouting made everyone miserable and that there were better ways to solve a problem. After the filmstrip, we tried to engage the kids in conversation about what they had learned. Winnie tuned us out totally. He pulled out a piece of paper and started to scribble. I made him put his paper away, but he continued to tune out everything. Wouldn't say a word to anyone.

You know, I think he figured out the filmstrip was directed at him. In fact, so did the other kids. During our discussion, one of my kids said that the boy in the filmstrip reminded him of Winnie. We could tell that the activity was beginning to upset Winnie, so we cut it short. So what do we do next? WHAT ON EARTH AM I GOING TO DO WITH THIS CHILD?

5/6

Wow! The gaps between entries just keep getting wider and wider. Well, the school year is about over and I must admit that I'm glad that the end is near. It's all been so very frustrating. You have so much ground to cover, your students are already behind all the other classes on your grade level, and you don't have time to teach anything because you're always dealing with some sort of behavior or attention problem. Still, I'll miss all of my kids a great deal, but I don't think I want this type of group next year--especially Winnie. If I got my class role for next year and his name showed up on it, I think I'd run out and jump off the nearest bridge. Even so, I feel that we did cover a lot of ground and that some progress was made. I had two students who we were able to get placed in the LD class for next year. Even though all of my students were ineligible for retention, I'm confident that most of them will do well in second grade next year. And yes, Winnie--even Winnie--made some progress. When he came to me he was a nonreader, but now he's the best reader in the class. One thing further. I learned so much from these kids and from Jackie this year. I know that my behavior management will be much better next year, and I know I'll be more competent at modifying curriculum to meet the needs of special students. So, I guess, in the long run, this has been a good year for me. Still, if the powers that be decide that I am to have another class next year like the one I had this year, I don't know what I'll do. If I have to deal with another Winnie, how on earth will I cope?

Part IV. Teaching Notes for the Cases

Precis for Each Case

WHAT YOU DON'T KNOW CAN HURT YOU! John McCullum
Precis. A student teacher in general education runs into problems with a class of diverse eighth graders when he tries to manage a group activity in his supervising teacher's absence, ending up in a protracted power struggle with one male student who, he later learns, has been in a class for students with emotional or behavioral disorders.

GRANDMA'S BOY: Helen Jamison
Precis. Part A: Early in her first year of teaching second grade, a teacher encounters difficulty in working with the father and grandmother of a boy who is having serious academic and behavioral problems.

Part B: With consultation from a school psychologist, the teacher attempts to use behavior contracts, but these are unsuccessful and result in the student's emotional outburst, leaving her feeling defeated.

IS KEVIN BLUFFING? Carol Yake
Precis. An experienced sixth grade teacher must deal with a crisis when one of her students, a boy diagnosed as psychotic but spending most of the school day in her regular classroom, appears ready to jump from a second story staircase.

THEY FAILED DERRICK: Melinda Smith
Precis. Part A: An experienced teacher of children with mental retardation, now teaching a regular fifth grade class, volunteers to take a student with a distinguished history of violent and threatening behavior, and now she must confront him about bringing a knife to school.

Part B: Although the teacher handles him masterfully, the student frightens the assistant principal and is placed first in a special class in a middle school and, later, in a mental hospital, leading the teacher to conclude that everyone has failed him.

THE FAIRY GODMOTHERS: Paul Miller
Precis. Part A: An experienced English teacher with a recent graduate degree in special education takes a mid-year position teaching 11-, 12-, and 13-year-olds with learning disabilities, discovers that the previous teacher apparently offered little or no effective instruction or behavior management and left her position precipitously, and finds that his aide and a young substitute apparently have only entertained the students with games for the previous three weeks.

Part B: Having taken over the class from the substitute, the teacher must deal with his students' use of racial epithets, their organized plan to test his instructional skills and authority, and a direct challenge from the group's ringleader.

THE PHANTOM PREGNANCY: Barbara Thompson

Precis. A regular classroom teacher struggles with how to respond to a 12-year-old girl in her class who, in addition to having learning disabilities and emotional or behavioral disorders, believes that she is pregnant from sexual abuse by her mother's boyfriend and insists that she wants to be sexually active and become pregnant.

STEALING TIME: Robert Carter

Precis. Part A: An experienced fourth-grade teacher who has a highly structured classroom that produces good results with many students with disabilities has increasing difficulty with a boy who has learning disabilities and problems with his peers, culminating in suspicion that he has stolen a classmate's watch.

Part B: The teacher determines that the boy has stolen the watch and must decide how to handle his continuing suspicion, and that of classmates, that the boy is stealing other items.

THE TRUTH ABOUT ALICE: Janet Lane

Precis. An experienced algebra teacher discovers belatedly that a rumor about an unattractive girl is contributing to her low social status, and in the context of apparent teasing by a group of boys the teacher wonders how she can help this student understand what is happening to her without eroding her self-image and social status even further.

ONE BAD APPLE: Elaine Brown

Precis. A veteran teacher, now teaching the group of fifth graders that she had in fourth grade, is confronted with problems created by two new boys, one of whom exhibits aggressive antisocial behavior, and soon finds herself enmeshed in coercive relationships with them as a means of maintaining her control.

THE CONTRACT WITH PARRISH AND SON: Rebecca Phillips

Precis. A middle school special education teacher finds that her typical behavior management system is insufficient for a new student, but her attempts to involve his father result in the student's apparent physical abuse, indications of depression, and a crisis in which he curses her and runs out of the room.

THE MASCOT: Cathy Anderson

Precis. A student teacher in a resource class for 11- to 13-year-olds with learning disabilities is kept in a subservient role by her supervising teacher, whose behavior management is questionable, and the student teacher finds herself in increasingly difficult circumstances midway through her eight week assignment.

WHOSE CLASS IS THIS? Jane Lee

Precis. Part A: A former special education teacher now teaching a regular fourth grade class has a continuing battle with a student's mother, who is a former teacher and sometimes serves as a substitute in the same school, over instructional and behavior management issues, culminating in the mother's direct attempt to dictate a behavior management strategy.

Part B: The teacher sends a letter to the mother, reasserting her professional judgment and authority, and is subsequently paid an unexpected visit by the father, a new school board member, which further shakes her confidence.

THE GHOST OF SCHOOL YEARS PAST: Jeannette Sloan

Precis. Part A: A first-year special education teacher in an elementary school finds herself a social outsider among the faculty, is constantly compared by her aide and others to her highly esteemed predecessor, who has returned to the university for a graduate degree, and eventually observes that her aide is not only usurping her authority in behavior management but questioning her decisions in discussions with other faculty.

Part B: The teacher confronts her aide, but subsequently discovers that her predecessor not only continues to influence her aide through frequent phone conversations but will be completing a practicum assignment in the school.

WINNIE: Patty Gray

Precis. Part A: A second-year teacher of at-risk first graders has particular problems with the behavior of one of her students, particularly his talking out and calling her name, and obtains help from a consulting teacher to develop a management plan, but she is not successful in resolving the problem by the Christmas holidays.

Part B: After school resumes in January, the teacher continues her efforts to resolve the child's behavior problems, including new strategies designed with the help of the consulting teacher, but she finds that the other students are beginning to imitate both him and her responses to him, and by the end of the school year she still has not found a solution.

YOU HAD BETTER GET ON THEM: Bob Winters

Precis. A teacher with formal preparation in early childhood special education assumes a position teaching middle school students with mild mental retardation and gradually looses all semblance of classroom control, ultimately lashing out at the students with unprofessional language and being confronted by the principal about his behavior.

We offer the following teaching notes for each case following a consistent format. First, we list the characters, followed by a brief summary of the events included in the case. Second, we highlight the special features we feel the case presents, although you may see additional or different features that you feel offer special teaching opportunities. Third, we comment on the teaching strategy employed by the central teaching character. Fourth, we outline "blocks of analysis" that, from our perspective, are major points that you might want to bring out in teaching the case. When a case has Parts A and B, we have treated the parts separately or together as seemed most appropriate to us. As we discussed previously, teaching with cases allows a great deal of room for creativity, flexibility, and personal judgment. Nearly everyone who prepares teaching notes will end up with the same list of characters and a similar summary of events. The other features of our teaching notes, however, represent quite subjective, but we hope helpful, perspectives on important issues.

WHAT YOU DON'T KNOW CAN HURT YOU! John McCullum

1. Characters: John, Student Teacher.
    Chris, Richard, Students.
    Mr. Roberts, Vice-Principal.

John attempts to review a test using a quiz-show game while his supervising teacher is out of the class. He allows the students to self-select and they do so according to ability and race lines. An argument develops between Chris (white, from the high-achieving group) and Richard, (black, low-achieving group). John manages to stop the squabble. After the lesson, John calls both students back to discuss the matter. Chris complies, Richard does not. John finds Richard at the bike rack and confronts him. Richard ignores John's attempt at conversation and leaves.

The next morning John takes Richard to the office. While waiting for the vice-principal, Richard whispers threats to John. This leads to another confrontation. John reminds Richard of his suspension after school that day, but Richard has an excuse. John decides to postpone the punishment to the following day. The next day Richard serves his detention but is disruptive and argumentative, even leaving the class. John sends for help to the office, and Mr. Roberts instructs John to release Richard from detention to avoid further problems. John is left frustrated and confused.

2. Special Features

Crucial to this case is John's turmoil about his predicament with Richard. John approaches Richard from several angles with little success. Decision-making is shown to be a tricky business, especially in view of the cumulative effects of earlier decisions. Each decision made by John shifts the focus of future events with Richard, setting these events in a definite direction.

John faces other issues such as:

2.1   loss of face with on looking students and staff members.

2.2   personal defensiveness about his decision-making.

2.3   feelings of powerlessness.

2.4   feelings of confusion.

2.5   intrusion of personal feelings into professional judgments.

2.6   John is white, Richard is not. John's reflections indicate that he is aware of this difference.

2.7   There is a communication problem between John and the rest of the staff. The vice principal does not communicate with John directly. Also, John relies on another teacher for help in getting information from the vice principal. This confuses referral procedures, resulting, finally, in John being faced with Richard when he was not supposed to be.

2.8   John is not familiar with the referral policies of the school.

John clearly tries his best to make the right decisions. He consistently sees the problem only from his professional, adult, personal point of view. Furthermore, John's decisions all revolve around each new crisis situation, and he tends to reflect only after times of emergency. His decisions are reactive rather than carefully considered beforehand. This crisis decision-making narrows his options and focus.

3.   Teaching Strategy

Teacher decision-making is executed repeatedly throughout the school day. These decisions result in immediate tangible results which are sometimes not what the teacher intended. Whatever the outcome, these decisions are nevertheless powerful influences on the students, the teacher, learning, and classroom management. Teachers must learn to "think on their feet' while simultaneously considering the impact of their actions on learning, school policy, the needs of the students, and their professional and personal worth.

This case illustrates the complexity of decision-making in the classroom, and how reflection, anticipation, and clear thinking are pivotal to ensure optimal student performance.

4.   Blocks of Analysis

4.1   Classroom Management: John is involved in several management issues:

4.1.1   Unexpectedly having students divide into teams along lines of ability.

4.1.2   Disruption caused by the quiz.

4.1.3   Having to intervene in the fight between Richard and Chris.

4.1.4   Dealing with the consequences of the fight.

4.1.5   Richard's sudden departure at the bike rack.

4.1.6   Richard's remarks to another student while waiting to see the vice-principal.

4.1.7   Richard's excuse not to come to detention.

4.1.8   Richard's behavior in detention.

4.1.9   John's decision to ask uninvolved students to retire to the library.

4.2   Decision-Making Processes: John makes multiple decisions that affect the course and final outcome of events. He struggles with his personal feelings, often allowing his personal attitudes to influence professional judgments. Do all teachers struggle with the interference of personal feelings? How are personal intrusions controlled or allowed for?

4.3   Richard's Motivations: While the case does not supply many details about Richard, his behaviors and reactions to John's decisions are evident. There are many underlying reasons why Richard reacts the way he does. Are underlying causes an excuse for oppositional behavior? Should these underlying reasons be considered when dealing with students who choose not to follow rules?

4.4   Teacher Preparation: The case suggests that John's decisions were not based on a pre-planned strategy. Rather, John's decisions were dictated by Richard's reactions and oppositional behavior. Was the "hit-or-miss" approach an unfortunate exception or had John's teacher training failed to prepare him? How can teachers be better prepared for what they might face in their first classroom?

4.5   Inner Reflection: John constantly debates whether he is doing the right thing. The case reveals John's deep reflection of what he is attempting to accomplish with one student and with the class as a whole. On another level the case illustrates John's desire to become a more expert teacher by being aware of the decisions he makes and his tenacity to find solutions. How can teachers be taught to reflect on their decision-making? How can teachers be made more aware of the effect of their reflections on their behavior?

4.6   Pre-emotive Solutions: At several points in the case, different decisions by John would have led to very different outcomes. How do teachers learn pre-emptive strategies that will support them in times of crisis? Can such skills be taught as part of teacher preparation, or is learning by experience the only way?

4.7   Winning Over the Student: John's course of action betrays a singlemindedness of purpose. There is little to suggest that he considered any other point of view than his own. Should teachers make decisions based on their perceptions all the time? What are the consequences for learning and classroom management in making decisions from the point of view of the students?

4.8   Status of the Teacher: John's decisions affect how he is seen by others, especially Richard. John quickly relies on the authority of the vice principal and the English teacher. Furthermore, John's supervising teacher has relinquished the control of the class, and therefore most of the authority, to John. While others provide temporary relief for the immediate emergency, John's reliance on others for authority has clear implications for his own authority and teacher status in the future. Should teachers rely on other professionals for authority and if so, how often? If a teacher has relinquished authority to others in order to manage a class, how can this be changed?

4.9   Teacher Liability: Richard engages in behavior which is potentially dangerous. Twice, John is separated from Richard while Richard is under John's supervision. If Richard had injured himself or others at these times, there is a possibility that John could be held liable for failing to properly supervise Richard. Where does the teacher's responsibility in such a situation end? How else could these events been dealt with?

4.10 Expectations: John has certain expectations for the entire class and for individual students. His expectations are not all met which results in confusion, anger, and frustration. How John deals with these emotions will have an impact on how he approaches similar situations in the future. How do teachers learn to match their expectations to reality? What skills do teachers need to help them cope with unmet expectations and disappointments?

4.11 Racial Overtones: John is white, while Richard is African-American. The issue of racial tension is probably present. In addition, Chris is white. How do teachers handle racial tensions, especially when they are implied rather than overt?

GRANDMA'S BOY: Helen Jamison

Part A

1.   Case Summary

Characters: Helen Jamison, Second Grade Teacher.
Cindy, Helen's Roommate and Confidante.
Justin Richardson, Student.
Judy, Justin's First Grade Teacher
Mr. Richardson, Justin's Father.
Mrs. Richardson, Justin's Grandmother.

Justin is not keeping up with the rest of the class. Justin's school records indicate that his behavior had deteriorated the previous year and that the first grade teacher had referred Justin for special services assistance. It appears that Justin is rather passive-aggressive. Helen decides to schedule a conference with Mr. Richardson, Justin's father. However, before she does so, she talks with Judy, who fills her in on Justin's background of divorced parents and a very strong-willed paternal grandmother. Judy also mentions that Mr. Richardson had denied the child-study team permission to test Justin the year before. Judy advises Helen to seek the support of other school personnel, but Helen decides to push on alone. Mrs. Richardson accompanies Mr. Richardson to the interview with Helen. The interview soon reveals that Mrs. Richardson is in control, and that she blames Justin's problems on his absent mother. Mrs. Richardson refuses to accommodate any one of the several suggestions made by Helen, insisting that all Justin needs is more physical punishment at home. Helen feels like a failure and is at a loss as to how to proceed with what is best for Justin.

2.   Special Features

Helen is facing a dilemma: She is acutely aware of Justin's withdrawn behavior, and knows that one key to addressing the problem is to obtain the support for her efforts from Justin's guardians. However, how to reach Justin while faced with active opposition from the child's home is something entirely unexpected.

Helen has a problem both with Justin and the family. This complicates matters greatly. Helen is a new teacher who is trying (and, to this point, has obviously succeeded) to create a favorable impression among her colleagues and superiors. Furthermore, this is her first real encounter with an openly oppositional family. Helen feels pressure to help Justin, but also wants Justin's home environment to be supportive of what she does.

3.   Teaching Strategy

All teachers are faced, sooner or later, with lack of support, and even hostility, from the home of a problem child. This is a very delicate matter. The teacher wants what is best for the child for the advancement of learning, and is aware of the child's behavior in class. There is no doubt that the student is faltering and needs help outside of the classroom. Not only is this an academic problem, but clearly, emotional and psychological concerns for the student pressure the teacher into some action. After consultation with colleagues who may know the child, the next

60

logical step is to elicit the support of the parents or guardians, or, at the very least, to alert them to the fact that their child is experiencing difficulty. Usually, parents are cooperative. Many inexperienced practitioners, take home support for granted. In this case support was not only denied, but Ann Richardson is openly hostile. Justin's family not only oppose any measures suggested by Helen, but suggest that Justin is to be punished for his lack of cooperation.

4.   Blocks of Analysis

4.1   Teacher Reactions: Helen reports several significant feelings in dealing with this situation, revealing the intricacy of her position from a personal and professional point of view. She feels that she is totally unprepared to deal with the situation, especially seeing that up to this point in her brief career, Helen is proud of the cooperative atmosphere that she has created in her class. Also, she focusses her feelings of sympathy on Justin, seeing the situation from his point of view. This appears to cloud her consideration of options. Helen enters the interview already having been subjected to Judy's opinions that this is, in all probability, a hopeless situation. Helen feels some guilt when it becomes apparent that Ann Richardson wants to beat Justin for the way he is behaving in school. Indirectly, Helen feels that calling attention to Justin's problems will result in punishment for Justin rather than assistance. Are these emotions appropriate and valid? Can they support or detract from her concern? How?

4.2   Family Dynamics: The Richardson family reflects the complexity underlying Justin's problems, specifically:

4.2.1   The divorce of Justin's parents.

4.2.2   The geographical move into Ann Richardson's house, in and of itself a traumatic event.

4.2.3   The dominance of Ann Richardson over both Mr. Richardson and Justin.

4.2.4   The passive acceptance of Ann Richardson's decrees by Justin's father.

4.2.5   Ann Richardson's attitude toward physical punishment for Justin's problems.

Is Helen trained to deal with these complexities? Why or Why not? Should she take them into account when attempting to find a solution that will best help Justin?

4.3   Consultation of Colleagues: Helen consults with Justin's former teacher in the hopes of obtaining some information to help Justin. However, she gets more than she bargains for: A very negative evaluation of Justin's homelife.

Did she do the right thing, so that in the interview she would be prepared for what was to come, or should she have interviewed "cold" so that previous reports of Ann Richardson would not have clouded her judgements?

4.4   Lack of Skills: Helen feels that she was unprepared for the interview in terms of:

  4.4.1   What to expect from Ann and Mr. Richardson.

  4.4.2   How to explain Justin's difficulties in a way that would convey concern, rather than Ann Richardson's perception that Justin was misbehaving.

  4.4.3   How to have drawn Mr Richardson out to the point where he, as Justin's father, could have given permission for Helen's plan of assistance.

  4.4.4   How to isolate Ann Richardson in the interview to where she no longer controlled it.

  4.4.5   How, perhaps, to compromise enough of what she had in mind for Justin so that Ann Richardson would have felt that she had "won".

Should teachers be trained to be, in effect, crisis counsellors so that they will possess the interpersonal skills needed in situations such as this?

4.5   Legal Implications: Justin has been denied access to special services because Mr. Richardson, probably at Ann Richardson's instigation, refused to authorize assessment procedures. Does this infringe upon Justin's right to services? Ann Richardson makes clear that Justin is to be physically punished as a direct result of the meeting. What recourse do teachers have when parents refuse permission for assessment? How does Helen judge whether she should inform her principal or child welfare authorities about these statements made by Ann Richardson?

4.6   Professional Pressure on Helen: Helen is aware of how much of an impression she has made in her short time as a teacher, in all the areas, apparently, that could influence her career in the future. The Richardson's problems, and Helen's feelings of inadequacy to find a solution, could show her up as not being as competent as here colleagues first thought. Should Helen take this into account when looking for other solutions?

4.7   Ann Richardson's Point of View: Ann Richardson is adamant that she understands why Justin is behaving the way that he is, and that she has been able to handle it effectively in the past. Could there be some truth to this? Could it be that Justin is simply an obstinate child angry at the divorce of his parents?

4.8   Acceptance of Reality: It appears that there is not much that can be done for Justin at present. Is there a point where a teacher must simply do the best for such a student while the student is at school and nothing more? Why?

<u>Part B</u>

1.   Case Summary

Helen's reflection compels her to seek assistance from other school personnel. The week after the meeting, she takes Justin's case to the child-study committee again, recommending that they try to approach Mr. Richardson one more time to get permission for testing. Instead, the committee recommends that Helen work with Ron Saunders to develop interventions that would increase Justin's cooperation and productivity. However, the situation deteriorates. Each behavior management strategy is defeated by Justin through manipulation, cheating and ignoring. Feeling frustrated, Helen decides to confront Justin about his cheating. Justin reacts angrily and barricades himself in the class bathroom. Helen judges that he is in no mood to leave. The class becomes agitated over this display of anger. Helen sends an SOS to Ron, who us able to diffuse the crisis. Later, Helen, Ron and the principal discuss the crisis and decide to refer Justin to the child-study committee for the third time. Helen is at the end of her wits, and is resolved that this time things will have to change.

2.   Special Features

By this point, Helen has gathered a great deal more information about Justin and his problems. Certain options Helen thought were available in part 1 of this case have been denied. Justin's family will not allow him to be tested; her efforts to get Justin to cooperate in class have been resisted; her teaching ability, so admired in her short tenure, has not helped here; Helen's frustration and helplessness are increasing. In addition, Helen seems unable to accept that Justin may not, in fact, be reachable.

Helen is becoming more personally involved, and relying more and more on her friend as a means of comfort and support. She realizes that she must enlist the aid of other professionals to deal with Justin. However, she also remembers that much is expected of her as the new 'star' teacher. Once Helen finally gets other professional support, she expects that the strategies that she and Ron devise will work. When they don't, Helen does not know where to turn.

3.   Teaching Strategy

Helen consistently vacillates between hopelessness and the hope of new strategies. She invests a great deal of her emotion in Justin, almost willing him to improve. When this does not happen, her resentment is clear. Helen is not in control of the situation, and she is painfully aware of this. When Justin's behavior deteriorates, she takes this as a failure of herself as a person and a professional.

Many teachers give up on a student when they feel that they can't make a difference. They feel that something they did in all of their laborious efforts should have helped. The perspective of the severity of the child's problems eludes them as they enter the vortex of self-recrimination and blame. Not only is this destructive to teacher morale, but it does not help the student.

63

4. Blocks of Analysis

    4.1 Acceptance of the Need for Help: Helen finally acknowledges that she needs the help of support personnel in her dealings with Justin. Up to this point she has been convinced that she could do it on her own. These feelings of independence were undergirded by the pressure she felt in being a new, promising member of staff, and the belief that she could make a difference in every student. Experienced teachers live up to their professional obligation to do their very best to reach all students in whatever ways they can, but thy also know that there are some students who, if not immune to assistance, require much more attention that can be given in a regular classroom.

    4.2 Deteriorating Circumstances: For much of the time Justin remains passive and calmly uncooperative. Helen is surprised when Justin acts out by yelling and hiding in the bathroom. Helen fails to see that this episode comes after Justin's other, less overt resistance is cut off by the implementation of the plans she and Ron discussed. It is useful for teachers to learn that student responses can change when previous inappropriate behaviors are limited, and that behavior changes will not always be what the teacher anticipated.

    4.3 Teacher Assumptions: This second part of the case reveals some assumptions under which Helen has been operating. She sees Justin as a child who "will not be broken." This perception explains some of her approaches, and that she sees Justin's undesirable behavior as something that must be destroyed. Also, she sees Justin as deviant from the norm: "I just felt like grabbing him by his shoulders and shaking some sense into him."

    4.4 Conditional Teacher Responses: Because Helen is so involved with Justin's lack of response to her hard work, she is personally offended when things don't go as planned. She feels that because of her hard work, Justin should be responding and be improving.

    4.5 Intervention Sequences: Helen and Ron approach Justin correctly. They decide upon an intervention strategy and put it into action. When the strategy is only partially successful, they modify their approach and try again, attempting to get closer to the perfect strategy to handle Justin.

    4.6 Teacher Discussion of Possible Other Consequences: Helen is alarmed at Justin's outburst and retreat to the bathroom. While Helen and Ron discussed interventions, they did not explore all the possible consequences that these interventions could precipitate. Teachers should be aware that interventions sometimes produce unexpected, and not necessarily welcome, behavior changes.

    4.7 Teacher Decisions in a Crisis Situation: Helen deals with Justin's outburst in an appropriate way, making the best of a difficult situation:

        4.7.1 She remains calm and maintains at least an outward sense of control. This is important for the onlooking class.

4.7.2   She opens the door as soon as possible to gain visual access to Justin, whose wellbeing is her responsibility.

4.7.3   Helen takes a short time to asses the situation and come up with a plan. She does not act in a "knee-jerk" way.

4.7.4   She realizes that she needs help and immediately calls for Ron.

4.7.5   Helen relinquishes Justin's care to Ron and attends to the rest of the class, deescalating a potentially disruptive situation.

4.8   Additional Professional Assistance and Interaction: Helen enlists the help of the school referral committee and Ron, the itinerant school psychologist. The results are less than encouraging. Helen is disappointed that the intervention suggested by Ron does not work. Is Helen's disappointment justified? Is it realistic to believe that outside expert help will improve Justin's behavior?

4.9   Alternative Strategies: Helen and Ron pursue alternative strategies when their initial efforts are unsuccessful. They continue to refine their approaches, meeting Justin's challenges one by one. What can teachers do when even their alternative plans are unsuccessful? How do teachers deal with students who exhaust the teacher's repertoire of responses?

4.10   Identification for Special Education: Helen is convinced that Justin should be identified for special education services. Should this happen, Justin will be associated with the label of a special education category. What are the implications for children identified for special education? Is identification and advantage or a hindrance to their academic, emotional, and/or psychological development.

4.11   Student Defiance: Justin's behavior becomes increasingly defiant. Helen faces a confused class and a tricky situation with Justin in the bathroom. Fortunately, the crisis is resolved. Could Helen have handled the situation any differently? Why/Why not? How can teachers plan for these kinds of eventualities?

IS KEVIN BLUFFING? Carol Yake

1.   Case Summary

Characters: Carol, Classroom Teacher.
                     Kevin, Student.

As in the past, Kevin is having a tantrum over some minor issue. Carol knows that the rest of the class are afraid of Kevin's psychotic outbursts, but at the same time she is determined not to let Kevin know that she is frightened, too. She remembers Kevin threatening to kick out a plate glass window and his history of physical violence toward her. Carol also knows that she spends a great deal of time hiding her fear and dislike of Kevin from him. She despairs of real support from home and feels alone in keeping Kevin from destruction.

Today is even scarier. As she stands frozen at the board, Kevin is precariously perched on the railing above the second story stair well. He is angry and threatening. She remembers Kevin's threat of suicide, and is more confused when one of her stunned onlooking students asks if Carol will be to blame if Kevin dies.

2.   Special Features

Carol is in a must-act position and there is very little room for error. At the same time, she knows that Kevin is probably threatening more than serious about suicide. Her dilemma is what to do in the next few seconds. Her professional responsibility compels her to prevent an accident yet she is too far from Kevin to grab him without him seeing her coming--something which might precipitate him jumping.

3.   Teaching Strategy

In dealing with students with behavior problems, especially students who are unpredictable and self-destructive and/or violent, teachers sometimes only have a split-second in which to react to avoid serous injury to themselves or their students. In many of these situations the entire burden for resolving the situation rests entirely with the teacher alone.

4.   Blocks of Analysis

    4.1   Dangerous Behavior: Kevin's behavior is not only extremely dangerous but is also an indication of his lack of appreciation of danger, to say nothing of being a good example of his self-destructive tendencies. How can teachers structure the behavior of such a student to lessen the risk of serious injury or death to the student? How can teachers teach students the implications of their dangerous behavior? Should there be punitive consequences for this type of dangerous behavior?

    4.2   Teacher Fear and Panic: Carol is afraid of Kevin's behavior and is constantly fearful of future outbursts. How can teachers cope with these stressful emotions when dealing with students with sever behavior problems? How do these emotions influence teacher decisions and judgements about managing dangerous or intimidating student behavior?

66

4.3   Student Unpredictability: Kevin's behavior outbursts are, at best capricious. How can teachers structure the classroom setting to lessen unpredictable inappropriate behaviors? What behavioral interventions are likely to lessen the frequency of unpredictable outbursts of inappropriate behaviors?

4.4   Placement: Due to administrative problems beyond her control Carol feels that it is her duty to help Kevin even although it is clear that his placement in her class in probably inappropriate. What can teachers do to protect themselves and other students from the dangerous behavior of students inappropriately placed in their classes? Should teachers accept students in their classes who are clearly in need of more intensive services?

4.5   Physical Restraint: From time to time Carol is forced to physically restrain Kevin. What skills do teachers need to learn in order to effectively restrain students exhibiting behavior that warrants restraint? How effective is physical restraint as a behavioral intervention? What are the consequences of physical intervention?

4.6   Child Abuse: Kevin has a history of child abuse. How much of his behavior can be attributed to his life history? Can childhood psychosis be linked to causal factors of child abuse? Should psychotic children be placed in regular classes?

THEY FAILED DERRICK: Melinda Smith

1. Case Summary

Characters: Melinda Smith, Teacher.
              Greg Rodgers, Principal.
              Derrick Yates, Student.
              Karen, Fifth Grade Teacher.
              Barbara Cole, School Social Worker.
              Doug, Assistant Principal.

Melinda Smith took a break from teaching special education to head a gifted class but found that her special education background followed her. Greg pleaded with her to enroll Derrick who had serious emotional problems and was underachieving. The previous year Derrick had been so disruptive that he had to be picked up by his mother most days at lunchtime. The entire staff waited eagerly to see how she would handle the terror of the school. Barbara Cole filled her in on Derrick's painful background, including the fact that Derrick had killed and mutilated the family dog. Derrick was so violent that he virtually ran his home. He had threatened his mother with a knife so often that she slept being a locked and bolted door.

Initially, Derrick didn't know how to handle the fact that Melinda didn't appear intimidated by his reputation so he set out to make matters right. Coming to school on the bus one morning he threatened several students with a knife. Melinda decided it was time to confront Derrick

After some scary moments, Derrick handed over the knife. In the ensuing days Derrick deliberately defied the rules of the classroom. Changing her strategy, Melinda tried ignoring and looking for any puny opportunity to praise Derrick. This strategy seemed to help, if only a little. However, Derrick found things too calm and took to physically intimidating students around him at every opportunity. Changing gears again, Melinda talked firmly with Derrick in the hall and demanded he apologize. It worked. By Christmas he was decidedly better and much more a part of the class. Better that is, until he held Doug hostage and had to be physically removed to the office.

Early in January, the child-study team recommended that Derrick be sent to a special school where he was to be classified as severely emotionally disturbed. Melinda couldn't help but feel that all her hard work had been wasted and that things might have been very different for Derrick if the team had given him another chance.

2. Special Features

The case illustrates a multifaceted set of problems for Derrick, Melinda, and the rest of the class. Derrick comes to the class with significant behavior problems and a reputation that has preceded him. Melinda views his presence as a challenge which can be overcome. She feels that had she been given more time even more progress could have been made. The school administration, however, does not see it this way and moves quickly after the bathroom incident to have Derrick removed form this class.

There are several matters of judgement involved in this case: that of the teacher in feeling that she could have handled derrick for the rest of the year, that of the administration and the placement team who think otherwise, as well as the initial decision to place Derrick in a class of gifted students in the first place.

Derrick's problems are seriously affecting his learning, social interactions, and his ability to make appropriate decisions for living and learning. The rest of the class are forced to accommodate his intimidating behavior for fear of reprisal.

In addition, Melinda feels that her "project' for the year has been wrested from her grasp and that her many years of experience have failed her. She is resentful of the role of the administration in giving up on Derrick.

3.   Teaching Strategy

Many teachers feel that they can accomplish more than is realistically possible with students with serious behavior problems. Judging the small success of children like Derrick, however, must be weighed against the effect of their presence on the rest of the class, how much he or she is actually progressing in real terms of learning and adjustment, and the wisdom of dealing with a violent student in a setting where, potentially, he or she may do a great deal of harm to fellow students and the teacher.

On the other hand, sometimes making any progress with a particular student is a breakthrough and the gained momentum is unlikely to be regained one the student has been removed from the class.

4.   Blocks of Analysis

4.1   Placement Team Decisions and Responsibility: Melinda is frustrated with the placement team for recommending that Derrick be placed in special education. We do not know if she mentioned her feelings in the placement meeting, but irrespective of what was said, the decision was clearly in favor of removal of Derrick from the class. When should teachers have the final say over whether a student leaves or not? What factors would argue for or against this position? Do placement teams always make appropriate decisions based on their "paper knowledge" of the student under review?

4.2   Realistic Appraisals of the Students' Presenting Problems: The case makes clear that the assessments of the team differ greatly from what Melinda believes. Who has the true picture of Derrick? How do teachers and teams bring greater parity to their assessments of students like Derrick? What evidence is needed for the most appropriate decision to be made with the smallest margin of error?

4.3   Efficacy of Intervention: Melinda is convinced that the placement team and the administration did not give Derrick enough time to improve. How do professionals decide how much time should elapse before an intervention is judged ineffective? What interventions with students with serious behavior problems have potential of being effective the longer they are in place? What interventions tend to work only in the short term?

4.4   Teacher Ownership: The case makes clear that Melinda shows a strong sense of ownership about Derrick. Does strong emotional teacher ownership of a student affect judgements concerning behavioral interventions or assessment of students progress?

4.5   Appropriateness of Intervention Strategies: One prior intervention was to send Derrick home after lunch. How appropriate are such interventions? What are the ramifications for student academic and social learning when extreme behavioral interventions are implemented?

4.6   Threatening Behavior: Derrick regularly threatens his peers and teachers. He appears to have built a reputation based on intimidation and manipulation. His threats mean that he misses many important school activities. How do teachers asses the seriousness of threats from students? How do teachers make judgements about whether student threats are genuine or simply manipulation? Should threats from students always be taken seriously? If teachers do take threats seriously, what procedures should be followed to insure their own safety and that of the students for whom they are responsible?

4.7   Homelife Influences: Derrick appears to be as difficult to handle at home as he is at school. His mother is at a loss to control him and fears for her life and the lives of her other children. At least some of Derrick's behavior seems to stem from his dysfunctional relationship with his father and his mistaken perception that his mother is preventing him from seeing his father. How much does Derrick's unstable homelife contribute to his behavior problems? Should teachers make allowances for students from unstable homes? How involved should teachers become in the homelives of troubled students?

4.8   Violent Behavior: Derrick is capable of extremely violent behavior. There is little guarantee that his history of violent behavior will subside. What kinds of services and placement arrangements are necessary for student like Derrick? Should school administrators assume that special education teachers, by virtue of their experience or expertise, will be able to cope with these students? What skills do teachers need to recognize the potential of violent behavior? What skills are necessary to contain violent student behavior if it erupts in the classroom?

4.9   Truancy: Derrick's progress is hampered by spotty attendance. He is able to remain home because of the fear he has instilled in his mother, family, and possibly previous teachers, who may have been only too glad when he did not arrive at school. What are the responsibilities of teachers when students are truant? Is there merit in ignoring truancy as a way of protecting other students from potential harm? What are the procedures that teachers need to follow in dealing with a truant student?

4.10   "Honeymoon Period": Derrick seems to be calm for the first few weeks of the year and Melinda correctly assesses that this is the "honeymoon" period where students generally are compliant until they have grown used to classroom routines. How can teachers accurately assess student behavior during this initial period? Are there behavioral indicators during this time that may later turn into major management problems? If so, how can teachers be alert for them?

4.11 Challenges from Students: Derrick challenges Melinda by reminding her of his prior reputation, hoping to engage her in a power struggle or argument. She manages to turn the encounter into a positive experience for Derrick. What other ways can teachers use to mold potentially negative confrontations with students into mutually satisfying experiences? Is this remolding always appropriate or desirable? What are the implications of confronting students who challenge teachers?

4.12 Weapons at School: Derrick threatens a student on the school bus and then brings the knife to class. What measures can teachers take to prevent students from bringing weapons to class? What is the best way of dealing with a student who is found to be in possession of a dangerous weapon? What is and appropriate consequence for a student found to be carrying a weapon?

4.13 Confronting a Student in a Potentially Volatile Situation: Melinda approaches Derrick and kneels by his side. She then gently confronts him about the knife. What physical proximity limits should teacher maintain when dealing with students known to be violent and be carrying a weapon? What are the consequences for the entire class if the teacher acts in a fearful or panicky manner? How can these situations be deescalated and satisfactorily resolved?

4.14 Explosive Behavior: Several times in the case Derrick demonstrates a capacity for explosive behavior that is difficult to anticipate. What is the best way to deal with explosive behavior? What possible consequences could result from explosive student outbursts.

4.15 Reinforcement of Appropriate Behavior and Shaping: The teacher deescalates Derrick's rage by skillfully reinforcing any appearance of desired behavior, in this case calmness. She does not insist that he become completely compliant immediately. Rather, she uses whatever compliance she sees to move Derrick away from agitation and towards control of his emotions. What strategies do teachers need in order to be successful in shaping student behavior? What are the disadvantages of implementing techniques of shaping?

4.16 Oppositional Behavior: Derrick's oppositional behavior is excessive. He leaves the classroom at will and is openly defiant. What are the most effective ways of dealing with oppositional behavior? Can teachers justify ignoring oppositional behavior? What are the most effective ways of reducing oppositional behaviors?

4.17 Second-Guessing Students: When Melinda confronts Derrick for leaving the room without permission she makes the decision to second-guess Derrick's motives for his inappropriate behavior. What motives could teachers have for engaging in "mind games" about the behavior of their students? How accurate is second-guessing in predicating student behavior?

4.18 Setting Consequences: When Melinda talks with Derrick about his unexcused absence from the room she skillfully states the consequences for future transgressions. What skills do teachers need to deliver consequences for inappropriate behavior in a clear yet nonthreatening manner? How do teachers deal with students who become resentful when consequences are delivered?

71

4.19   Teacher Tenacity: Melinda displays great tenacity in refusing to be defeated by Derrick's oppositional and explosive behavior. She repeatedly attempts different strategies when old ones are no longer effective. How do teachers know when to remain tenacious? How do teachers make the decision that they have done everything possible to help a student, and that there is no more that they can do to improve student behavior?

4.20   Preparing the Student: Realizing that Derrick is volatile, but also feeling the need to enforce some consequences for his inappropriate behavior, Melinda prepares him for what he must do once he reenters the classroom. She states clearly that he must apologize and then tape the paper he tore back together again. What are the difficulties teachers encounter in preparing students for the consequences of their behavior? How can teachers prepare student for the sometimes unpleasant tasks they must face for misbehaving?

4.21   Speaking with the Rest of the Class: Melinda enlists the help of the class in dealing with Derrick's behavior problems. Is it appropriate for teachers to deal with students' behavior by enlisting the help of the rest of the class? When is it acceptable or desirable to use peer pressure to modify behavior, and when is manipulation of peer pressure unethical?

4.22   Teacher Awareness: In the midst of all her other duties, Melinda, displaying almost a sixth sense, realizes that Derrick has been out of the class longer than usual. How do teachers develop this apparent sensitivity to the setting of the classroom? How do teachers learn to remember so many classroom issues simultaneously?

THE FAIRY GODMOTHERS: Paul Miller

1. Case Summary

> Characters: Paul Miller, Teacher.
> Jane Abbot, Principal.
> Irene Walker, Aide.
> Mrs. Flint, Teacher.
> Cathy Hansen, Substitute.
> Mandy, Paul's Predecessor.
> Glen, Brian, Randy, Shane, Cynthia, Students.

Part A

Paul takes over a self-contained special education class in the middle of the year. Paul learns from the principal and Irene Walker that Mandy, Paul's predecessor, had difficulty controlling the class. Apparently, Mandy, in a desperate effort to regain control, had resorted to some rather questionable tactics. When these failed, she resigned abruptly and made sure that everyone, including the students, knew why.

Paul senses that things are less than organized. His uneasiness is exacerbated when, on the first day of classes, Cathy Hansen arrives to teach having not been told that Paul is assuming responsibility for the class. Paul, however, is prepared for the students and impresses them by calling them by name when they first enter. He is confused when Cathy remains in the classroom and proceeds with morning routines as if he wasn't there.

2. Special Features

Paul has accurately gauged the situation he will face when the students arrive. He knows that there will be several major changes needed before he will be able to control all of the activities in the classroom. Based on the information provided by Jane Abbot and Irene Walker and in conjunction with what he discovers about Mandy's teaching from what she leaves behind in the class, he is determined to make some necessary changes. However, he is not prepared for Cathy Hansen's appearance, nor for the curious behavior she displays by remaining in the class and continuing to act as if she still has some responsibility--in spite of his very clear statements to her. Paul sees the students gravitating to Cathy, and he realizes that his newly-won, if minimal, status with the students is in jeopardy.

3. Teaching Strategies

Many teachers find themselves in difficult situations when they take over classes in the middle of the school year. These teachers inherit classes who already have been molded, for better or for worse, by the previous teacher. Often, the new teacher has a different teaching approach and management style to their predecessor which may make the period of mutual adjustment longer and increase the potential for conflict. The new teacher faces another area of potential conflict in dealing with staff who know the previous teacher. These people can have a great influence on the new teacher's ability to effectively manage the class and individual students. The new teacher must often expend a great deal of energy to carefully evaluate the situation and use it to the greatest benefit for effective classroom management.

4.   Blocks of Analysis

4.1   Inappropriate Levels of Textbooks: A common mistake make by special education teachers is their selection of textbooks which, while at an appropriate reading or comprehension level, may appear, to the students, to have "childish" or boring content. Some teachers, for example, see nothing amiss in assigning a children's book to a junior high school student with reading problems. Such inappropriate assignments can cause embarrassment, despondency, and apathy among students who are acutely aware of their academic shortcomings. How can these issues be avoided? Should they be avoided? Is it ever appropriate for teachers to assign books which, while academically at the appropriate level, are inappropriate for the chronological age of the student?

4.2   Information from Staff Regarding a Predecessor: Paul gathers a great deal of information from the staff about his predecessor which leads him to a set of decisions about how to manage the behavior of the students. Most incumbent teachers will receive such information either implicitly or overtly. In this case, it appears that Paul accurately evaluates what he is told. However, it could have equally been the case that the information he received was erroneous, which would have resulted in negative consequences from the beginning. How much should new teachers rely on information about their predecessors to guide their classroom management decisions? How can incumbent teachers judge the accuracy of the infirmation they receive? Should new teachers pay any attention to such information at all?

4.3   Students Leaving Class Without Permission: Irene tells Paul that students would often leave class without permission and Mandy would have to roam the halls and the school grounds looking for them. How can teachers avoid this situation? What aspects of behavior management can prevent these situations? What can teachers do when these situations occur in spite of preemptive measures designed to avoid them?

4.4   Confrontations With Staff in the Presence of Students: Mandy yells at Irene in front of the class when Mandy gets frustrated and is unable to handle the class. Is this teacher behavior ever acceptable? What are the ramifications for the teacher, the aide, and the students in terms of behavior management issues?

4.5   Inappropriate Language: Mandy becomes angry and bitter when she finally loses control of the class and resorts to foul language. Is foul language ever appropriate for teachers? What if foul language used by the teacher means that they can be more effective managers of their students' behavior?

4.6   Physical Confrontation: Mandy finally ends up in a physical confrontation with one of her students. When are physical interventions appropriate and necessary? When are physical interventions completely inappropriate? What criteria can teachers use for decoding when physical intervention is appropriate and/or necessary?

4.7   Intervention by Other Staff: It appears that the principal and other higher authority personnel do not intervene in Mandy's chaotic situation in spite of being aware of the situation. When is it appropriate for principals and other superiors to intervene in

74

similar situations? What are the responsibilities of school administrators and senior teachers in these situations? Are there situations where intervention by the principal is inappropriate or appropriate?

4.8   Teacher Anger: Mandy makes sure that her class is the object of her bitterness when she resigns. What are the problems associated with such inappropriate outbursts in terms of the class, the new teacher, and for behavior management of students who have been subjected to this level of unprofessional behavior?

4.9   Student Background: Cynthia appears to be a student who comes from a difficult home situation, yet, at school, she is compliant and isolated. What can teachers do not to overlook students like Cynthia, who often receive less attention because their emotional maladjustment is not overtly aggressive or noticeable?

4.10   Preemptive Measures: Paul prepares several measures ahead of time that he knows will help his students adjust to him and he implements them quite effectively. How can teachers evaluate their new setting and prepare ahead of time to ensure that their initial meeting with a new class will set the tone for their personal approach of behavior management?

4.11   Professional Power Plays: Cathy clearly ignores the fact that Paul is now in control of the class by acting as if she was in charge. How do incumbent teachers deal with these situations in order to assert their authority?

4.12   Emotional Involvement: Paul surmises that Cathy is trying to make up for the way they were treated by Mandy. What should teachers do when they take over a class that has been poorly handled by the previous teacher? Is it acceptable to attempt to "make up" for the inconsistencies or injustices of the past? What are the possible consequences of this approach in terms of student learning, effective teaching, and appropriate behavior management?

1.   Case Summary

Paul handles Cathy's behavior by getting Irene to talk to her about who is in charge. Cathy is reluctant to leave and only does so after extracting a reluctant promise from Paul that she can return to visit. Turning back to the class after Cathy leaves, Paul sees that Irene is unable to control the students and immediately corrects the lapse. He gets Irene to teach while he assesses students individually. Paul also does this as a way of getting to know each student a little bit better.

Paul begins to feel that he is making headway right from the start. He is encouraged further when his plan to get the class to take turns talking appears to work. His mood changes, though, when, after school, Irene tells him that the students, led by Shane, are planning a "revolt."

The next day Paul, aware of the possibility of conflict, compromises by letting the students continue their early morning routine of playing games while he attends to some administrative tasks. Later in the morning Paul returns to the classroom to find Brian and Vincent embroiled in an argument with Irene standing ineffectively by. He quickly settles the dispute, but later in the day Shane become openly insulting--an action clearly supported by at least some of the other students. Paul is left feeling angry and less in control than he had hoped to be.

2.   Special Features

Paul gets off to good start by accurately assessing the situation he will face when the class arrives. He spends time reflecting on the emotional climate of the classroom and does his best to anticipate the course of events that his arrival is sure to precipitate. For the first part of the day, this seems to work. However, by lunch the storm appears to be brewing. Once more, Paul tries his best to anticipate what is to come by adjusting his behavior management strategies. This buys him a little time, but by the need of the day his best efforts are not enough to prevent a blatant challenge to his authority.

3.   Teaching Strategies

Effective teachers spend a great deal of time reflecting on their actions and the results these actions have on their students. Effective behavior management requires constant adjustment to the mood and learning needs to both the teacher and the students. The more teachers think through their approaches to managing behavior in the classroom, the more likely it will be that they will be effective in controlling the learning environment. However, few teachers are able to anticipate every possible potential behavior management problem. Teachers must prepare themselves for the eventuality of facing problems and conflicts which they could not possibly have anticipated.

4.   Blocks of Analysis.

   4.1   Authority by Proxy: Paul uses Irene to convey his message of authority to Cathy. How does this action enhance Paul's status with Cathy, Irene, and most importantly, the students? What factors precipitated such a decision? What are the possible implications of such actions in terms of effective behavior management?

4.2   "Laying Down the Law:" Contrary to the actions of many experienced teachers, Paul refrains from explicitly telling his class right from the start what he expects from them to avoid a rebellious reaction. For most teachers, is this a good decision? What are the advantages and disadvantages of immediately informing a new class about rules? When is the best time for a teacher to introduce an implement their own set of rules for the class?

4.3   Teacher Reflection: Paul spends a great deal of time reflecting on the behavior of his students and his implementation of behavior management approaches. How important is it for teachers to reflect on their actions and the consequences of their behavior management approaches for their students?

4.4   Student Interruptions: Paul has a plan for dealing with students calling out in class. Is this approach always the best to manage this specific management problem? What other approaches can teachers use to teach students to speak in turn to increase effective communication? What can teachers do when their specific approaches are ineffective or detrimental to classroom behavior management?

4.5   Compromise: At several points in the case, Paul compromises his expectations in order not to "rock the boat." Is this approach appropriate in the context of the case? What are the benefits and constraints of this idea in terms of classroom behavior management?

4.6   Handling Student Conflicts: Paul manages to deal with the argument between Brian and Vincent effectively. What alternative approaches would have been equally effective? What approaches would have made the situation worse?

4.7   Deliberate Challenges from Students: Shane's challenge to Paul's authority is deliberate and well thought out. Paul recognizes this and is left feeling confused. How can teachers handle such deliberate challenges to their authority in such a way that they do not alienate the student while at the same time maintaining the locus of authority?

THE PHANTOM PREGNANCY: Barbara Thompson

1.   Case Summary

Characters: Barbara Thompson, Teacher.
              Teri Leigh, Student.
              Bob Farris, Principal.
              Marge Thurman, Assistant Principal.
              Kay Middleton, Special Education Teacher.

Barbara has mixed thoughts about how her class will react to the new Family Life Curriculum which she must teach. She is especially concerned about the effect on Teri Leigh seeing that Teri has a history being sexually abused. Teri's history of LD and psychoses doesn't help matters at all. Several weeks into the class Teri begins to fantasize about being pregnant. Barbara counsels Teri by trying to approach the problem in as many ways as she can. She gets the feeling though, that Teri hasn't heard a word.

Shortly after the discussion, Teri gives some high school boys on the school bus several nude pictures of herself. Bob Farris ascertains that Teri's foster mother had directed Teri, and her foster sister, who had taken the pictures, to destroy them. This obviously didn't happen. Bob Farris and Marge Thurman felt that Barbara was the best one to counsel Teri about this episode.

In discussing the episode with Teri, Barbara learns of the connection between Teri's fantasy and the pictures: she had given the photos to the boys because she wanted to have sex and get pregnant. Teri feels that having sex is the best way to get popular with boys. Barbara talks to Teri about the responsibilities of having children, and the possibility of communicable diseases. Teri will have none of it--she insists that she wants a baby. Nothing seemed to help. Barbara feels helpless and ineffective.

2.   Special features

Students with mild handicaps display a wide variety of inappropriate behaviors. These behaviors are not limited, for example, to routine classroom misbehavior, but may, as in this case, encompass inappropriate social activity. This situation is aggravated by the student's inability to "read" social cues and to make appropriate decisions about sexual matters.

Barbara Thompson faces a series of difficult circumstances in dealing with Teri. She has appropriately anticipated that the new sex education curriculum would present difficulties for her special students. Teri confirms this suspicion. Barbara is acutely aware of the ramifications of Teri's obsession with getting pregnant, and yet Barbara realizes that there is a good chance she is being totally ineffective in steering Teri in a different direction. She is also struggling with a school system that appears to be "passing the buck," and abdicating most of the responsibility for Teri to Barbara.

3.   Teaching Strategy

Barbara's predicament is less usual than many other behavior management problems faced by teachers. Very little in her experience as a teacher or in her training could have prepared her for this situation. She approaches the problem based on experience in other areas, hoping that these tactics will suffice. Her personal feelings as a mother become intertwined with her professional obligations and Barbara feels out of her depth to make any bigger difference in Teri's life.

4.   Blocks of Analysis

    4.1   Sex education curriculum: Sex education curricula are a feature of many school education programs. In some communities their presence is hotly debated and many teachers are uncomfortable addressing sexual behavioral issues. Unlike most academic subjects, sex education courses are not adapted for the needs of students with mild handicaps. How much do students with handicaps actually learn from these programs? How are attitudes towards sex influenced by a student's mild handicap?

    4.2   Separation anxiety/abandonment: Teri's past has been traumatic. Her history of abuse has engendered deep feelings of insecurity and a strong desire to be loved at any cost. Teri Leigh uses inappropriate means of attracting attention in the hope that she will find the security and love she so desperately seeks. How can Teri be directed toward more appropriate means of emotional gratification especially seeing that she already has learned that the promise of sexual favors is a powerful way of attracting attention?

    4.3   Childhood psychosis: Psychotic behaviors are more serious and unusual than many other behaviors that teachers deal with. Teri's fantasies and aggressive sexual behavior are part of her psychotic disposition. Is Barbara's class a suitable setting for Teri? Is Barbara equipped both professionally and emotionally to deal with psychotic behavior?

    4.4   Inappropriate attention-seeking: Teri seeks attention in inappropriate ways. One problem with some inappropriate attention-getting behavior is effective in getting attention. Teri has learned that she can get the attention she seeks immediately and at will. How can teachers redirect students to more appropriate attention-seeking behaviors when some inappropriate behaviors are so powerful?

    4.5   Timing intervention decisions: Throughout this case there are times where professional interventions can be made. How do educators decide on the timing of interventions that will be in the best interest of the student? How do teachers decide which interventions will be most effective and which may be harmful in delicate situations such as this?

    4.6   Inter-agency cooperation: Clearly Teri Leigh's problems require the intervention of several social service agencies. What are the teacher's responsibilities in dealing with other agencies for the benefit of the student? Should Barbara refer Teri to other agencies or the school counselor?

4.7   Student inability to understand behavioral consequences: Teri does not fully comprehend the consequences of the choices she is making. She is unable to establish adequate cause and effect relationships in her behavioral choices. Barbara tries her best to explain these links to Teri, but to no avail. How can teachers teach students with mild handicaps to see the causes and effects of their behavioral choices?

Part A

1. Case Summary

Characters: Robert Carter, Regular Class Teacher.
                    Lisa Griffith, Special Education Teacher.
                    David, Student.
                    Bob, Student.

Robert runs his class strictly, setting the rules at the beginning of the year and expecting each student to do their best. David, an LD student, attends his class for nonacademics. After Christmas, however, David enters Robert's class for math, science, and health. David does not complete his work, becomes disruptive and belligerent and disturbs the well constructed harmony of Robert's class. As David's behavior worsens, Robert's resentment and anger grow. During group work, David refuses to cooperate and the group grade suffers as a result. As a consequence, David becomes isolated from his peers.

One day David refuses to work, claiming that he wants to return to his self-contained class. He complains that his peers in the regular class dislike him. Robert confronts his misbehavior as the reason for their dislike. After lunch that same day, David's behavior escalates to the point where he is removed to the principal's office. Later David and Robert discuss David's behavior and reach a shaky compromise which lasts for a few days, after which David continues to act out.

In David's absence, Robert and the class discuss David's behavior. Robert quickly manipulates the situation to where they all agree that David is the villain.

One afternoon Bob's watch disappears. The next morning David proudly announces his ·
acquisition of a watch from his dad--a watch that looks exactly like Bob's. Robert, and many in the class, feel that this is no gift, but Bob's misfortune.

2. Special Features

This case demonstrates the complexity of both personal and professional interaction between a teacher and his students. It shows how easily personal anger and rigidity can turn very quickly into a situation where there is almost no chance for an amicable, professional and humane solution. Robert's highly structured classroom is disrupted by David's increased presence, and Robert will not tolerate any rocking of his carefully sailing boat. David must comply or face very serious consequences.

Robert is fixed on solving the problem with David in a strictly defined way, and seems to be oblivious to other alternatives. David is convinced that his behavior is justified, and he will not concede defeat, instead escalating his opposition. The rest of the class is acutely aware of the drama being played out before them, and also of Robert's feelings and biases towards David.

3. Teaching Strategy

There is a dividing line between personal feelings and professional decisions. If these boundaries are crossed, order, trust, and the teacher/student relationship can be damaged. All teachers face a student that "pushes their buttons"--a student who will test capabilities to the limit, and, sometimes, push the teacher beyond reasonable solutions and negotiable outcomes. Allowing feelings of anger and defensiveness to be communicated to onlooking students can compromise teacher status, efficacy, and the ability to manage a classroom efficiently.

4. Blocks of Analysis

4.1 Sudden Change in Student Behavior: It is clear that David's behavior changed suddenly and markedly. Just as clearly, there is a possibility that the deterioration in David's behavior is directly linked to his removal from the learning disabilities class. Could this situation have been avoided by preparing David for the change? If so, how could this have been accomplished?

4.2 Teacher Perceptions of Student Behavior: Robert perceives David's lack of cooperation in a very narrowly defined way. After all his hard work at structuring his class and creating an efficient learning climate, David poses a danger of destroying it all. Should Robert change his perceptions? Should David be made to conform? If David is made to conform, will David's attitude necessarily improve?

4.3 Deterioration of Social Interactions: David's behavior disturbs the rest of the class. As David continues to defy the norms of the class, he becomes increasingly isolated and, in the view of his classmates, strange. This exacerbates an already tenuous situation. Does noncompliance with class norms always result in isolation of the problem student? Is it possible to reduce isolation while the student is still displaying inappropriate behaviors? Why?

4.4 Appropriateness of Contingencies for Misbehavior: Robert swiftly imposes a series of limits and consequences upon David for his lack of cooperation. The limits seem to be the same limits that teachers have imposed upon students for centuries. Could Robert have dealt with this issue differently? What other strategies could he have used to get the results he wanted?

4.5 Teacher's Handling of Crisis Events: It appears that Robert acts quickly and, at least in part, out of his personal feelings and frustration with David. He appears hurt that David will not comply. He does not reflect upon what might occur, and prepare himself accordingly. His "knee-jerk" reaction in literally removing David from the desk is questionable. How do teachers prepare for crisis situations? Is it possible to prepare for these events? If so, how?

4.6 Teacher as Precipitator of Student Problems: Part of David's inappropriate behavior results from Robert's handling of key issues. Robert appears very rigid in his approaches and almost entirely unwilling to compromise his strict guidelines. Teachers need to be aware that their behavior can precipitate not only positive reactions from their students, but also negative reactions which may have unforeseen, costly, consequences.

4.7   Escalation of Inappropriate Student Behavior: David's behavior does not change and then remain constant at a new level. It continues to escalate in spite of the limits imposed by Robert. There is every chance that this will continue. How can Robert reverse this trend? What strategies would be most effective with David and the rest of the class?

4.8   Teacher's Physical Intervention: Robert physically removes David from his desk. In most communities, physical interventions by a frustrated or angry teacher are frowned upon. Also, there are many legal ramifications of Robert's actions. Teachers must weigh carefully their actions when physically intervening with their students and be fully aware of the implications for their actions for themselves as well as for others, including the school, school system, and the community.

4.9   Student Manipulation of Teacher: David is not blameless in this setting. He demonstrates several highly manipulative behaviors in dealing with his fellow students and with Robert. What do students accomplish from manipulative behavior? Is David justified in these behaviors under these circumstances? Why/Why not?

4.10   Use of Cooperative Techniques With Uncooperative Students: Robert's entire class is built around the concept of cooperative learning, which presupposes that all students are willing to work as part of a group and for the benefit of a group. David obviously does not agree. How does a teacher deal with a student who does not fit into the overall plan of the class? Should Robert change his class routine for David? Should David be made to comply? What if David continues to be unmotivated, and some other students fail because of David's actions? How will Robert explain such ramifications to other parents?

4.11   Power Struggles for Control of the Class: Robert is determined to win. So is David. Both feel that they have just cause for their perceptions. In this struggle, there has to be a winner or loser. How can a loss for either side be avoided?

4.12   Discussion of David With the Rest of the Class: Robert discusses David with the rest of the class without David being present. He attempts to explain his position, and appears to feel justified in his use of physical force against David. Robert clearly takes the class' side against David. Is this fair to David? How should teachers deal with honest questions from students about their classmates? Should a teacher ever side with one student against another? Why/Why not? If this event was relayed to David's parents, how do you think they would react? What are the legal implications of this type of teacher behavior?

4.13   Trust Between Teacher and Problem Student: The episode with the watch appears to confirm Robert's biases toward David. How fairly can he deal with this situation? What can Robert do to improve this situation?

4.14 Stealing: Children steal for a variety of reasons. In part B of the case, it becomes clear that David's stealing will be a chronic problem which will probably complicate future classroom situations. How do teachers need to handle stealing in the classroom? Should stealing be handled differently for special education students than for their regular class counterparts? Should students who chronically steal be treated differently than students who steal only once?

<u>Part B</u>

1. Case Summary

Robert gets David to hand over the watch. David denies that he stole the watch. Robert, David, and Lisa meet in the principal's office to discuss the matter. David repeatedly denies that he stole the watch, even when threatened with a call to his father. Robert calls David's mother first, who tells a different story of what David told her about the watch. David is pressured once more, and finally admits to stealing the watch. Returning to class, Robert insists that David apologize. He does so half-heartedly, and Bob remains angry.

Later, it turns out that the principal does not punish David for the theft. Soon other items start disappearing from Robert's class and it's clear that the rest of the class suspects David every time. Robert feels that he has failed to resolve this very serious situation.

2. Special Features

Robert is sure that David has stolen the watch long before the evidence is gathered. His approach is carefully measured to achieve some very specific goals:

2.1 To get David to admit his wrongdoing.

2.2 To return the stolen property.

2.3 To insist that David apologize to Bob.

2.4 To check out all the possibilities that may indicate that David was telling the truth.

2.5 To let David know that stealing is unacceptable, and that all the members of staff agree with him.

2.6 To make David realize that dishonesty requires restitution.

Robert is angry when David refuses to confess. He feels that he is spending too much energy in trying to right the situation. While he is weary from the constant battle, he is prepared to stick with it until David owns up. He realizes that his feelings toward David are changing, and he feels that David is adding to this by his lack of cooperation. Furthermore, later in the case, Robert is puzzled by the lack of response from the principal.

3. Teaching Strategy

Student dishonesty can quickly become a frustrating quagmire, even for experienced teachers. Sometimes getting at the truth is impossible. Teachers must develop strategies for these situations based upon the severity of the problem, the policies of the school and school district, and their personal feelings toward lying.

4. Blocks of Analysis

    4.1 Student Dishonesty: David's dishonesty was easy for Robert Carter to see in spite of
         his protestations of innocence. It takes a great deal of effort by Robert and Lisa
         Griffith before David relents. At each point in the escalating pressure, Robert gives
         David a chance to "come clean". Escalating pressure can also be useful in other,
         similar, situations.

    4.2 Occasional vs. Chronic Lying: It becomes apparent that David's lying is habitual and
         part of his repertoire of inappropriate behaviors. Is this any different from the
         behavior of children who lie once in a while when they find themselves in difficult
         situations?

    4.3 Team Approach: Robert enlists the aid of Lisa Griffiths and the school principal to
         get to the bottom of the problem. It is doubtful whether David would have confessed
         had Robert tried to do this on his own. Team approaches can be very effective in
         dealing with student dishonesty and manipulation, provided the team members have a
         good working relationship and that they are all familiar with the student.

    4.4 Asking: Why?: Robert asks David why he is behaving the way he is, and he receives
         a predictable answer: shrugged shoulders. Many students do not know why they
         behave the way they do. Questioning them about their motivations for lying is often
         fruitless and frustrating.

    4.5 Connection Between Behavior and Restitution: David knows that he must apologize,
         but he has little idea why this is necessary. He fails to see the connection between
         his actions and their consequences. Robert does not address this issue. David's
         confusion increases when his apology to Bob causes an angry reaction.

    4.6 Role of the Principal: There is no action or explanation from the principal. Stealing
         is a serious offense, and some action from the administration is anticipated by Robert
         and Lisa. What message does this convey to the teachers and to David and Bob?

    4.7 Self-Fulfilling Prophecy: Later in the year David automatically assumes blame when
         things go missing. How can Robert change this attitude in himself and his students?

THE TRUTH ABOUT ALICE: Janet Lane

1.   Case Summary

Characters: Janet Lane, 9th/10th Grade Algebra Teacher.
               Alice, Algebra Student.
               Martha Keys, Guidance Counselor.
               Mitch, Algebra Student.

Janet teaches Alice, one of the most physically unattractive students she has ever seen. Alice dresses poorly, is overweight, and has poor personal hygiene. Alice is also a weak student although she was removed from the school's LD program at her parents' request. After the first few days of class, Alice begins coming late to the after-lunch class each day. Janet is prepared to excuse this infrequently but as this becomes a regular habit, Janet is forced to confront Alice. Alice insists that she has no choice but to be late for class. Janet is mystified about Alice's reaction and seeks assistance from Martha Keys. Martha knows what Alice's problem is and gleefully recounts the details to Janet.

Alice has become the laughing stock of the school since the year before when she was seen brushing her teeth in the toilet bowl of the girl's restroom. Apparently, Alice's mother had insisted that Alice brush her teeth every day after eating her lunch. The problem had previously been solved by Martha giving Alice permission to brush her teeth privately. This explained why Alice is late for class. Janet now understands the class reaction to Alice when she enters the class late each day.

The class reaction continues as the weeks wear on, and Janet chides them for their insensitivity. Things improve for a few days, but then Janet becomes even more upset when she intercepts Alice's enthusiastic reply to a "love note" from Mitch, the ring-leader of the group who spend most of their time ridiculing Alice.

2.   Special Features

Janet Lane's predicament illustrates the nature of adolescent peer dynamics and the inability of some students to cope with the adolescent social environment. The case reveals how difficult it is for some learning disabled students to make appropriate choices in their actions, decisions, and basic best interests.

Janet's efforts are, at best, weak. She is empathetic, yet is unable to provide any meaningful relief to Alice. Janet's attempts to use her authority as a teacher to solve Alice's personal problem of embarrassment, rejection, and emotional pain. Janet attempts solutions without a firm grasp of the situation. Her inattention to "what's going on" make her ineffective and more of a hindrance than a help.

3.   Teaching Strategy

Teachers sometimes confuse their professional responsibilities with personal feelings. They also experience feelings of protectiveness towards students who are isolated and made fun of. Many professionals have had not training in how to deal with the sensitive issues demonstrated here. How do teachers help socially isolated students to become part of the group? How can teachers influence the peer group towards greater acceptance of the socially isolated student?

4. Blocks of Analysis

4.1 Unattractive Student Appearance: Every teacher encounters a physically unattractive child. Often these students have much more than physical unattractiveness going against them, including low academics, few friends, and an inability to relate at an age-appropriate level. Also, adolescent development dictates a preoccupation with physical appearance. A high priority is placed upon physical attractiveness. Unattractive adolescents may sense that they are at a disadvantage. What else could Janet have done? Were her actions well thought out and in Alice's best interests?

4.2 Removal of Alice From the LD program: Alice's parents removed her from the LD program in order that she might not be labelled LD in high school. This may be a poor choice on their part. Insisting that Alice be in a regular setting might have exacerbated Alice's academic problems and also increased her social isolation. Alice displays serious academic problems as well as a lack of social understanding and foresight. This is a problem often faced by teachers. When do teachers know when to inform parents of the problems that their children are facing?

4.3 Teacher Authority: Initially, Janet accepts that Alice is going to be late and does not require any kind of explanation. Janet's behavior condones Alice's tardiness because she does not ask for an explanation for the lateness or at least grant permission after finding out the reason. Later Janet "puts her foot down" and indicates that the lateness must cease. Janet is surprised that Alice reacts strongly. Should teachers expect students to be compliant after allowing them greater freedoms that what should have been allowed?

4.4 Teacher Unmotivated to Seek Information: Janet clearly refrains from seeking information both about Alice's past history and the reason for the tardiness. When Janet finally discovers some very important information, she is forced to revise her approach. Furthermore, her changes in strategy are limited by not knowing about Alice's history. Is it realistic for teachers to "discover" their students or should teachers learn as much as they can in advance?

4.5 Reaction of the Guidance Counselor: Most teachers, especially counselors, are privy to a great deal of sensitive information about problem students. Martha Keys' reaction to Janet's questions is inappropriate. How should sensitive information about students be handled? How do teachers control their personal feelings and reactions when they are aware of potentially embarrassing situations that students may have experienced? What are the appropriate behaviors that teachers must display when discussing student problems?

4.6 Family Pressures Acted Out at School: Alice is reluctant to disobey her mother in spite of tremendous social pressure to dissent. She feels caught between parental authority and the ridicule of her peers. There are many family dynamics that influence children and Alice chooses ridicule rather than disobey her mother. This, along with the parents insisting that Alice not be in the LD class provides important clues to stressful situations within the home. Teachers need to be aware of the "bigger picture' outside of school and the influence that has on in-school behavior.

4.7   Reactions of the Class: The other members of the class react in a predictable adolescent way. The are fascinated by the offensiveness of Alice's actions and lack empathy for her plight. Brushing teeth in the toilet bowl is an action that most adolescents would not easily forget. The negative attention increases Alice's social isolation. Furthermore, due to the nature of Alice's indiscretion, there is a great deal of peer pressure for members of the class not to befriend her for fear of being labelled by those who disapprove of Alice and her behavior. How do teachers deal with students who are being ostracized by the rest of the class? What are the ways to encourage the establishment of positive social relationships for all students?

4.8   Student Reaction to Teasing: Alice repeatedly reveals that she is socially unable to cope. She feels peer pressure but is unable to make appropriate decisions. Alice realizes that she is socially isolated and feebly attempts to gain acceptance by feeding in to the behavior of the three boys who are making fun of her. Furthermore, she appears to be unaware that the boys are making fun of her or at least that she is willing to be made fun of if it means a chance for gaining acceptance. What can teachers do to teach socially appropriate skills and decision making?

ONE BAD APPLE: Elaine Brown

1.   Case Summary

Characters: Elaine Brown, Classroom Teacher.
William, Student.
Eddie, Student.
Jerry West, Visiting Teacher.
Mr. Paine, Williams Father.
Katherine Ellis, Teacher.

William transfers into Elaine's class and is an immediate problem. He works below potential in most of his work and for the first few weeks of school refuses to do math. He is also absent two or three days every week. Jerry goes to see Mr. Paine at work about the truancy problem. Jerry learns that Mr. Paine supervises Williams' getting to school as best he can, but because of his long works hours, it is impossible to ensure that William gets to school.

William's behavior becomes increasingly unpredictable and violent, apparently without provocation. One day William slams his books down very forcefully on Chuck's desk. It is clear that Chuck could have been hurt. Elaine decides not to let William provoke her into a confrontation.

On a day when William is absent, Elaine discusses his behavior with the class, feeling that her bond with them makes discussing William easier. She wants them to heed her warning to "walk on eggs" in an attempt to avoid provoking William.

The only student who does not seem to realize that William is a menace is Eddie. Eddie has difficulty connecting his actions to subsequent consequences. One day Eddie gives William a playful push while standing in line. In the ensuing struggle, William pins Eddie face-down, his knees firmly embedded in Eddie's back, pulling Eddie's arms upward as hard as he can. Elaine manages to end the fight, asking Katherine Ellis to watch her class while she gets William taken home. Elaine resolves later conflicts between the two by taking Eddie into the hall where she pretends to spank him. Eddie's feigned cries seem to appease William, and Elaine hopes that with this strategy she can survive the year.

2.   Special Features

Teaching experience does not always help in the classroom. However, experienced teachers are more likely to know what to do based on other similar encounters they have had in the past. While some aggression is common among children, Elaine's situation is particularly worrisome in that William's outbursts appear to be quite unpredictable. Furthermore, Eddie's presence and apparent lack of self-preservation makes a tough situation that much more threatening.

This case involves three distinct views of the world that are in conflict with each other. William has learned to solve problems and deal with his emotions by physical violence and intimidation. William clearly associates his intimidating behavior with getting what he wants. Eddie, on the other hand, is socially imperceptive and insensitive to the feelings of others. Eddie fails to relate the consequences of his behavior to the outcomes it produces. Elaine Brown expects students to do their best while realizing that they all have individual strengths and weaknesses. This combination of perceptions provides potential for many difficult situations in the classroom.

3.   Teaching Strategy

Violent behavior in the classroom is a well documented phenomenon. Even in young children aggressive outbursts can be frightening and intimidating. There is also great potential for physical harm to other students and the teacher. Legal ramifications must also be considered. Furthermore, teachers frequently deal with students who seem intent on provoking the classroom bully. How should teachers handle these outbursts? What can be done to avoid such occurrences? What do teachers look for that will warn them that an outburst is imminent? What are the emergency priorities when violence is happening?

4.   Blocks of Analysis

4.1   Teacher Expectations: Elaine approaches her students in a particularly mature way. She expects them to do their best and to give her the standards of performance she sets. However, she is aware that each student is unique, and she makes allowances for their individual strengths and weaknesses. It is clear that both William and Eddie give her less than she expects from them. How do teachers deal with students who give less than they have the potential to provide? Should teachers modify their expectations of performance when what they expect is not forthcoming?

4.2   Family Dynamics: There are several issues that may explain William's inappropriate behavior at school. William had previously experienced problems and had been identified as behavior disordered. There are indications that William's mother could not cope with him and sent him to live with his father. Mother's sporadic employment indicates a domestic instability. Did William's background cause him to experience behavior problems? Are disadvantaged students more often labelled as being behavior problems? How much should teachers allow for student's background to influence their judgements and expectations for performance in the classroom?

4.3   Withdrawal From Special Education: William's mother insists that he not be placed in a special education class, even although it is apparent that he has difficulty relating to his peers in the regular classroom. Students in need of help can be highly disruptive in an inappropriate classroom setting. What should teachers do? Why are some parents reluctant to allow their children the opportunity for special education services? What legal recourse do teachers have to get students help when parents forbid it?

4.4   Student Refusal of Work: William blatantly refuses to even attempt some of his work. What is the best recourse for teachers when faced with students who are uncooperative, especially when it is clear that there will be no support from the student's home? How can teachers motivate students to attempt work they find threatening or overwhelming?

91

4.5   Student Absences: Missing school over an extended period of time is detrimental to the progress of the child. Lack of continuity and routine is disturbing for the child, the teacher, and the rest of the class. However, when William's background is taken into account his truant is hardly surprising. How can teachers ensure that students attend school regularly? If William was forced to attend school on a regular basis, would his performance and behavior improve or would he be resentful of having to comply with a clear set of rules. What action can be taken against parents who condone the absence of their children from school? Should anything, in fact, be done?

4.6   Violent Student Outbursts: Displays of physical violence are upsetting to the perpetrator, the victim, and the audience. William's unpredictability makes for a great deal of caution and nervousness among his peers (except, apparently, for Eddie) and for Elaine Brown. Everybody in the class begins to "walk on eggshells" in case they inadvertently trigger some inappropriate reaction in William. William is aware of his power over the class and manipulates the situation at will. How can teachers modify the classroom climate in such a way that the potential for acting out will be lessened while at the same time being supportive to the student displaying the inappropriate behavior? What should teachers do if, in spite of their best efforts, an outburst occurs? What type of planning should be done in advance of these situations to ensure maximum safety and/or response?

4.7   Teacher decision Making: Elaine makes some difficult decisions in this episode. She makes many of her decisions based upon her philosophy of expecting a great deal from every child, but also demonstrates an ability to "think on her feet" in a crisis situation. How can educators learn to make appropriate decisions in the "heat of battle" to the benefit of all involved? How do teachers prioritize the order of decision-making in a crisis setting?

4.8   Discussion of Student with rest of Class: Elaine discusses William's inappropriateness with the rest of the class. Her motivation for doing this is to ease tension and to head off the chance of conflict. In many ways this is an appropriate decision, as it allows effective preparation of the students for future situations, alerts them to the fact that what they do may have an effect on others, allows them to rehearse appropriate coping skills, and molds a supportive environment. On the other hand, is it appropriate for teachers to talk about a problem student without the student knowing, especially when the conversation involves the student's peer group? Can teachers find alternative ways of preparing a class for a troublesome student?

4.9   Student Self Destructive Behavior: Eddie's failure to understand that he is endangering himself is clear. Eddie does not perceive the force of William's outbursts, even after experiencing them first-hand. Children who fail to learn from their mistakes can be extremely problematic for any classroom teacher. Eddie's insensitivity adds another burden to the already precarious class dynamics. How can teachers remove such a student from imminent danger? How do we teach children to profit from their errors when they are apparently unable to do so?

4.10 Teacher's Ignoring of "Vigilante Justice": Elaine feels that Eddie gets the treatment he deserves when he is physically rebuffed by his peers. However, Elaine does not ignore William's brand of "Vigilante Justice." Do teachers deliberately send mixed messages to their students? Are mixed messages ever appropriate in dealing with children? Is it possible to teach without giving children mixed messages? How much inconsistency on the part of teachers is permissible? Is inconsistency permissible at all? Should teacher inconsistency be avoided at all costs?

THE CONTRACT WITH PARRISH AND SON: Rebecca Phillips

1.   Case Summary

Characters: Rebecca Phillips, LD Teacher.
               Bob Parrish, Student.
               Mr. Parrish, Bob's Father.
               Mr. Moore, School Psychologist.

Bob continually undermines Rebecca's group contingency behavior plans by drawing attention to himself through inappropriate language and general noisemaking. Rebecca eventually places Bob on an individual contingency program in an effort to stop him losing points for his workgroups. Knowing that Bob has a tough homelife, Rebecca sets up a meeting with Mr. Parrish. Rebecca and Mr. Parrish agree on a home behavior contract with Bob. Rebecca reports misbehavior to Mr. Parrish as part of that plan. However, each time this happens, Mr. Parrish beats Bob. Bob became resentful, blaming Rebecca for the beatings he is subjected to at home.

Bob's helplessness and resentment continue to grow, and Rebecca refrains from reporting misbehavior to Mr. parrish, fearing that Bob will be beaten again. However, Bob's behavior gets so out of hand, and Rebecca so angry, that she finds herself threatening Bob with his fathers' beatings if he does not toe the line. Bob becomes more compliant, and the next day Rebecca sees him writing angrily in his journal. Despite the confidentiality of the student journals, Rebecca feels she needs to see what Bob has written. It is a note suggesting that he may be thinking of suicide. Rebecca reports the note to Mr. Moore.

Mr. Moore recommends that Rebecca observe Bob closely before any action is taken. Bob becomes disruptive and Rebecca, angry once again, threatens Bob with his father. Bob encourages her to call his father, expressing the hope that his father will kill him. Angry and hurt, Bob rushes from the room.

2.   Special Features

Rebecca is fighting an uphill battle--not only with Bob in the classroom, but with his father. Mr. Parrish's perceptions of authority and parenting make it difficult for her to make any headway. Bob is caught in the middle, knowing that his behavior in class will be sure to bring down his father's wrath at home but also knowing that he can use his father's behavior against Rebecca. Bob blames Rebecca for his father's abusive treatment. As the situation escalates, Rebecca becomes enveloped in some of the helplessness felt so keenly by her troubled student.

Rebecca is in a difficult situation. Her class, except for Bob, works well under the new group contingency behavior management plan. Isolating Bob on an individual plan has not worked, and instead of Bob seeing his father as supportive, Bob is afraid and helpless. Bob sees Rebecca in collusion with Mr. Parrish against him, and this perception escalates his noncompliant behavior.

Rebecca wants to help Bob, but it seems that her efforts backfire and reinforce Bob's impressions. The suicidal note and drawings are real enough but Rebecca is not sure whether their intent is genuine or whether they are simply another exotic attention-getting ploy. Mr. Moore, the counsellor, appears ineffective and ignores the urgency of the situation by recommending observation and recording of any untoward behavior from Bob. Rebecca realizes that if the suicidal notes are serious Bob is in danger and needs more urgent intervention.

3.   Teaching Strategy

Dealing with students like Bob is extremely difficult. The forces acting in the classroom and in the student's homelife influence teacher behavior management options. Rebecca would have a whole different set of options to manage Bob if his father's outlook about Bob's behavior were different. Within these restrictions, Rebecca must walk a fine line to avoid invoking Mr. Parrish's wrath towards Bob, her classroom management goals for this student, and the risk of alienating Bob for good.

4.   Blocks of Analysis

   4.1   Use of Group Contingency: Managing classroom behavior is often effective when using group contingencies. Peer pressure can be a productive tool not only for behavior management but for teaching cooperation and important social skills. However, these approaches depend on the willingness of each student to agree to the limits and conditions of the group contingency. Some students may refuse to cooperate, and the teacher must then find an alternative solution which will be effective not only with the refusing student but also with the rest of the class. What criteria should teachers use to select their behavioral approaches? How much of their selection depends on the students and how much depends on personal teacher preferences and strengths?

   4.2   Negative Attention: Many students with mild handicaps are adept at gaining negative attention through their inappropriate behavior and manipulation of teacher and peer emotions. In this situation, refusing to be part of the group is highly effective in manipulating Rebecca's behavior towards Bob. Bob's self-destructive behavior escalates by provoking the involvement of his father, who he knows will be abusive. This, in turn, manipulates Rebecca to more negative action towards Bob. How do teachers end this cycle without losing more behavioral control? How do teachers become aware that sometimes students are controlling them more than vice versa?

   4.3   Student's Previous History: Rebecca is well aware of Bob's past behavior from his file but she tries to not hold that against him in the hope that he has changed. How much was Rebecca's attitude influenced by what she had read about Bob? If a teacher knows that a new student has a history of behavior problems, is it fair to wait and see what happens? Would Bob have been better served if Rebecca had set up a plan for Bob before he arrived? Would she have been able to handle Mr. Parrish differently if she had spoken with him before the crisis emerged?

   4.4   Double Entendres: Students often pick up on ambiguous meanings in what teachers say, and, especially in adolescence, tend to capitalize on these opportunities to make jokes. Sometimes these comments can be extremely embarrassing to the other students and the teacher alike. How should teachers handle these instances? Is it best to ignore them and keep teaching, or is it more effective to address them to prevent future occurrences?

4.5   Singling Out One Student: Singling out students who are behaving inappropriately is sometimes effective in modifying behavior. What are the ramifications of recognizing one student as separate from the rest of the class? In the long run, what are possible consequences of this teacher behavior?

4.6   The Influence of Homelife on School Behavior Problems: Many students demonstrate problem behaviors in school that are, at least in part, a product of relationship dynamics at home. Teacher actions in managing behavior in the classroom can have unanticipated consequences for students at home. To what extent should teacher behavior management decisions be influenced by the home situation of the student? What approaches can teachers use to increase the likelihood of cooperation from the parents or guardians of their students?

4.7   Student Manipulation of Teachers: Some students blame teachers for things that teachers have no control over--in this case the father's behavior. In an attempt to gain negative attention students sometimes weave elaborate networks to play teachers against parents, peers against the teacher, and so on. How do teachers learn to spot these behaviors among their students? How do they separate manipulative behavior from genuine student issues that should rightly be addressed by any professional teacher?

4.8   Suicidal Ideation: Students who display suicidal ideation sometimes frighten teachers. Teachers are often not sure of their role in dealing with suicide threats or notes. They may feel confused or that dealing with suicidal students is not part of their job. On the other hand, most teachers would not want to be responsible for a student coming to any harm. How do teachers deal with student suicidal ideation? How do teachers distinguish between genuine threats, pranks, or the use of suicidal ideation as a manipulative tool? What support systems are available to teachers in schools to cope with this situation?

4.9   Escalation of Inappropriate Behavior: Most teachers have experienced an escalation of inappropriate behavior in a student in spite of their best efforts to control the situation. Often the increase of inappropriate behavior is rapid and unpredictable. How can teachers best prepare for these instances? What emergency steps can teachers take to buy time and calm things down? What are the best ways to prevent possible physical violence and injury?

4.10   Students Leaving the Classroom: Teachers are well aware that they are professionally and legally responsible for their students. What can teachers do when an agitated student suddenly leaves the room, effectively removing him or herself from the teacher's control, but not the teacher's responsibility? Are teachers liable for injury to students who leave their rooms without permission? What can teachers do to prevent this situation from occurring?

THE MASCOT: Cathy Anderson

1.   Case Summary

Characters: Mrs. Clem, Classroom Teacher.
            Cathy Anderson, Student Teacher.
            Jabar, Student.

Cathy looks forward to her teaching practicum until Mrs. Clem, in front of the class, tells her that she has passed muster with the boys as "good looking". It turns out that Mrs. Clem sees the class as her family and is very possessive and controlling. Sarah feels unwelcome and isolated from the students--Mrs. Clem sees to that. Most of the time Cathy is a one-dimensional aide, given menial duties like being line leader.

When Cathy finally gets to teach, she senses that Mrs. Clem's earlier remark has lost her respect with the boys. In a science lesson, Mrs. Clem does everything she can to interrupt, including correcting students in the class while Cathy is teaching and "forgetting" to bring things she promised for Cathy to use in her lessons. Cathy becomes exasperated when Mrs. Clem unexpectedly asks her to teach lessons without prior notice. When Mrs. Clem gives some erroneous information to the students Cathy feels helpless to correct the situation.

Cathy needs a special science kit for her lesson. Mrs. Clem assures Cathy that she would get the kit from her car at lunchtime. The kit isn't there when Cathy needs it. In spite of her anger Kathy tries to settle the class and deal with this unexpected event. Mrs. Clem interrupts again, undermining Cathy's authority. In desperation, Cathy reminds Mrs. Clem about the kit. It becomes clear that Mrs. Clem expects Cathy to get the kit. To make matters worse Mrs. Clem insists that Jabar accompany Cathy. Cathy had already chosen someone else, as Jabar had misbehaved earlier in the day. In getting the kit, Jabar refuses to comply with any of Cathy's directions, instead running ahead of her back to the classroom. When Cathy gets to the classroom, Mrs. Clem has already directed Jabar to set up the kit. By this time Jabar is acting out and ignoring Cathy in spite of her pleas for order. Finally, Cathy restores order, only to have it destroyed again by Mrs. Clem yelling at various students from the back of the class.

As the practicum goes on it is obvious that Jabar is playing Cathy against Mrs. Clem. Cathy feels helpless. Jabar is Mrs. Clem's favorite and can do no wrong. Cathy feels she has lost a student and that she has been betrayed by her supervising teacher, someone she wanted to be her greatest ally.

2.   Special features

This case illustrates how student misbehavior can be a direct result of a power struggle between a supervising teacher and a student teacher. Cathy continually runs up against the controlling efforts of Mrs. Clem who appears to have an agenda of her own that is not supportive of Cathy. Jabar is a favorite student of Mrs. Clem, who persistently overlooks his inappropriate behavior. Instead Mrs. Clem blames other students and by implication, Cathy. Cathy is anxious to do well in her practicum, and she struggles to gain respect from the class, a task that is all but impossible because of Mrs. Clem's constant interference.

97

3.   Teaching Strategy

Student teaching is usually a difficult time for a student teacher. However, many student teachers see their practicum as a very worthwhile learning experience. Students teachers, though, sometimes assume that their supervising teacher will be supportive, helpful, and generally their mentor. In instances such as the one in this case, this is not true. Some teachers resent the inconvenience of hosting a student teacher and some teachers are very possessive of their classrooms and students.

4.   Blocks of Analysis

4.1   The Line Between the Professional and the Personal: Mrs. Clem reveals many of her personal feelings and experiences with her class. She also shows strong ownership of her students by referring to them as her "family." Where should teachers draw the line between their personal and professional lives? How much, if anything of their personal lives should teachers share with their classes? Is it ever appropriate to discuss with students the difficulties involved with teaching, and what a burden teaching can sometime become?

4.2   Personal Comments About Another Teacher: Mrs. Clem makes it clear that she is the conduit for boys' approval of Cathy's appearance. Later in the case, Mrs. Clem again makes reference to Cathy's physical appearance to the class. What are the ramifications of this type of teacher behavior? Are compliments of one teacher to another in front of a class acceptable? How do these kinds of behaviors influence classroom behavior management?

4.3   Personal Agendas: Mrs. Clem clearly has a different agenda for Cathy than Cathy assumed. Mrs. Clem is also unpredictable and inconsistent in dealing with Cathy. Instead of findings support, encouragement, and assistance from Mrs. Clem, Cathy is foiled by passive-aggressive inconsiderate behavior by Mrs. Clem. Under these circumstances what are Cathy's options to make it through the practicum successfully and with her enthusiasm for teaching still intact?

4.4   Teacher Inconsistency: Mrs. Clem is inconsistent in her dealings with the students, especially those student who are her favorites. Mrs. Clem appears to have two sets of rules, one for the class and one for her "pets." How does teacher inconsistency contribute to behavior management problems? How can Cathy adjust to this situation in a way that does not cross Mrs. C. and yet remain true to her teaching ideals?

4.5   Power Struggle: Mrs. Clem sees Cathy as a threat to her teaching territory. She wants to be sure that Cathy will not usurp her authority at any time so she undermines Cathy's efforts to be an effective student teacher. Cathy is angry and frustrated, but she is not sure how to proceed. How do student teachers handle power struggles with more experienced colleagues? How do power struggles among teachers affect the behavior of the students they teach?

4.6   Interference of the Supervising Teacher: Mrs. Clem persist in interfering. She interrupts Cathy by yelling at students, demanding that students write apology notes in the middle of Cathy's teaching time, and insisting on favors for her "pets" by overriding Cathy's authority in front of the students. What are the consequences of these teacher behaviors for student behavior management? What do students learn from observing these kinds of situations?

4.7   Student Manipulation: Jabar understands that he is one of Mrs. Clem's favorites, and that he can use his position to go against Cathy. How can teachers avoid being manipulated by students especially when they have very little real power in the classroom?

4.8   Reinforcing Inappropriate Student behavior: Mrs. Clem's favoritism clearly reinforces some inappropriate student behavior. Does student favoritism always lead to inappropriate behavior? If not, why not? Are there instance where favoring one student above others is desirable or even preferable?

4.9   Lack of Student Supervision: Mrs. Clem allows students to leave the class when they are angry and to return of their own volition when they have calmed down. What responsibility do teachers bear for supervising their students at all times? What are some possible consequences of allowing students to leave the classroom voluntarily without supervision? Is this appropriate in some situations more than in others?

WHOSE CLASS IS THIS? Jane Lee

Parts A and B

1. Case Summary

Characters: Jane Lee, Fourth Grade Teacher.
Ann Dean, Fourth Grade Student.
Belinda and Art Dean, Ann's Parents.
Jim Black, Principal.

Jane is in her first year of teaching a regular fourth garde after several years in special education classes. She gets on well with Ann, but Belinda is becoming more of a problem as the year progresses. Jane is unwillingly pulled into a political fray with Belinda who appears intent on running the class for Jane.

The first sign of trouble is when Belinda complains about the switch in the reading curriculum but Jane dismisses this as a justifiable complaint. To make matters worse, Belinda acts as a substitute teacher in the school and appears to be dissatisfied with any number of situations. Jane soon receives another complaint from Belinda when an aide mistakenly assigns classwork for homework but Jane manages to smooth things over.

A little while, later Belinda, after substituting in another fourth grade class, openly makes disparaging comments about the state of affairs in the school. Jane remembers that Art has just been appointed to the school board and was probably hearing all the negatives news at home.

Belinda soon complains, about Ann's lack of participation in the reading fair, even although she was removed from the activity for another voluntary class. Jane is angry that Belinda does this in front of other staff members. Belinda, seeing that she is not getting the reaction she wants, insinuates that Ann is unhappy in class because of Jane. Jane remembers previous incidents where Belinda had marshalled support among parents against the school and teachers. She is angry and more threatened.

Several other incidents occur such as Belinda attempting to start what she feels is a positive reward system in Jane's class. The final straw for Jane is when, in spite of Jane's rebuttal, sends colored pencils to school for Jane to use as part of the reward system Belinda wants to seen in operation. At the end of part A, Jane considers her options before writing a letter to Belinda.

In Part B, Jane writes a firm letter to Belinda refusing to cooperate. She feels relieved that the matter is settled and she can resume teaching without further interference. Her relief is short-lived, however. A few days later Art Dean appears unexpectedly at the school to observe Belinda's teaching.

2. Special Features

Parental political maneuvering may have significant outcomes for teachers and the behavior of their students. In the battle for the control of the class, Ann has the opportunity to observe a classic power struggle between two authority figures. Although there is little direct evidence in the

100

case, these events certainly have some influence on Ann's behavior. Jane is trapped in what appears to be a no-win situation. If she relents, her status and professional integrity will be seriously damaged. If she refuses to go along with Belinda's wishes, she runs the very real risk of school board action instigated by Art.

3.   Teaching Strategy

Teachers often face parents like Belinda Dean. Ignoring the power of such parents to influence decisions, especially at the individual school level is unwise. The tactics employed by parents such as Belinda and Art Dean are well known to their children and usually at least some other parents and children in the class. This can lead to inappropriate student behavior and a direct challenge of the teachers' authority.

4.   Blocks of Analysis.

4.1   Interfering Parents: The case makes clear that Belinda feels she has a right to dictate what happens in Jane's class--not only with Ann, but with the class as a whole. Belinda's persistence reveals a drive to gain control and to "show who's boss." How can teachers prepare for parental challenges to their professional integrity and classroom authority? Do parents have the right to dictate what forms of behavioral management are used in their children's classes? What are the consequences of parental involvement in classroom management decisions?

4.2   Parents as Substitute Teachers: Belinda provides an essential service to the school through her substitution activities. Her presence in the school makes her privy to the daily routines and problems faced by any school and thereby give her a greater opportunity to be critical. Sometime she substitutes as the teacher in Ann's class. What effects on the behavior of students generally, and the substitute's children in particular, can a parent substitute teachers have? What possible behavior management problems can arise from these arrangements?

4.3   Politics and Behavior Management: There is every chance that most of the students are aware of at least some of Belinda's actions. The students may even sense that Jane is losing control of the class and that Belinda is the real power broker. If this is the case, what possible consequences could emerge in the behavior of the class towards Jane?

4.4   Appropriate Times for Dealing With Parents: In several instances Belinda deliberately chooses an inappropriate time to make her negative remarks in spite of Jane's attempts to steer Belinda to some private discussion. How can teachers preempt such situations? How should teachers deal with parents who insist on confrontation in front of other teachers or students? What possible behavior problems can arise when students witness confrontations between parents and teachers?

4.5   Parents Blaming Teachers for Their Child's Problems: Belinda clearly insinuates that Ann's unhappiness is Jane's fault. How do teachers decide whether such claims are valid? What should teachers do if such allegations are valid? What is the teachers' course of action if these insinuations are invalid?

4.6   <u>Using the Child as an Intermediary</u>: Belinda uses Ann as an intermediary to Jane in situations where there is the chance that Belinda and Jane may actually be able to talk one on one. Such behavior is common knowledge to experienced teachers. Both teachers and parents sometimes use students as intermediaries for a number of plausible or devious reasons. When should students be used as intermediaries between parents and teachers? What are the ethical limits of these delicate situations?

4.7   <u>Direct Parental Interference</u>: Belinda clearly oversteps the bounds of good taste and directly interferes in the running of Jane's class. Furthermore, the case implies that Art Dean is about to become involved. How much direct interference in professional decision-making should parents have? How do teachers learn to set limits on parents who insist on personally intervening in behavioral management decisions?

4.8   <u>Teacher Responses to Parents</u>: Belinda and Jane communicate through a series of letters to defend their positions. Is written communication appropriate in this case? When is written communication appropriate? When should direct communication (such as a conference) be used instead?

THE GHOST OF SCHOOL YEARS PAST: Jeannette Sloan

1.   Case Summary

Characters: Jeannette Sloan, Special Education Teacher.
                Christine, Karen, and Joan, Special Education Teachers.
                Cynthia Hudson, Jeannette's Predecessor.
                Pat Hughes, Previously Cynthia's, and now Jeannette's aide.
                Mr. Owens, Principal.
                Carrie, Student.
                Judy Rowe, 4th Grade Teacher.

Jeannette Sloan is a new special education teacher thrilled to finally be teaching. She does her best to fit in and to get to know her colleagues both in special and regular education. Initially, it is easier to get to know the other special education teachers, but Jeannette has increasing contact with the regular education teachers because many of her students are mainstreamed. Naturally, they ask her for advice about the special students they teach. She quickly finds that most of the teachers on staff are part of a closely knit social community. Furthermore, her predecessor, Cynthia Hudson and Pat's aide (who is now Jeannette's aide) were close friends.

Soon, when Pat disagrees with Jeannette's teaching decisions, Pat is quick to remind Jeannette that "Cynthia would have done things differently." The situation is complicated by the principal and other teachers all referring to Cynthia as a "wonderful teacher." Jeannette soon finds herself conforming to Pat's suggestions about behavior management--management that Cynthia used to impose and that Jeannette is not comfortable with. Jeannette senses that the power base has moved to Pat and that her authority as a teacher is being undermined. Even Joan mentions it one day. The situation become intolerable for Jeannette when Pat and Judy Rowe thinly disguise their ridicule one of Jeannette's teaching decisions.

THE GHOST OF SCHOOL YEARS PAST: Jeannette Sloan

<u>Part B</u>

Jeannette is left defeated when she confronts Pat, who brazenly admits to the ridicule. Jeannette tries to assert her authority but realizes that her position is weak. To make matters worse, Jeannette learns that Cynthia will be returning to the school to complete a practicum as part of her mater's program.

2.   Special Features

Jeannette has gotten herself into a weak position through Pat's manipulation and intimidation. She has been struggling to adjust to her first year of teaching while at the same time trying to become part of the school team. This has proved more difficult than Jeannette anticipated. Clearly, she has gotten into a power struggle not only with Pat, but with the unseen and unknown Cynthia.

The situation is complicated by the principal's comments and she feels bereft of any support to improve her lot. Cynthia has taken on mythic proportions and Jeannette sees herself as the victim. Her anxiety is increased by the knowledge that Cynthia, with her hefty reputation, will soon be returning to the school.

3.   Teaching Strategy

There is more to teaching than the students and their learning needs. The power relationships among members of the staff are often connected to behavior patterns among students, who are acutely aware of teachers who have power and authority and those that do not. These situations are exacerbated when a member of staff such as a teachers' aide appears to have more authority and expertise than an inexperienced teacher. This setting is immeasurably worsened when a previous teacher has been held in high esteem by the entire school culture. How do teachers like Jeannette overcome these odds? What are the ramifications for student behavior if such a situation continues? How conducive are such situations for learning and effective teaching?

4.   Blocks of Analysis

    4.1   <u>Power Struggles</u>: Often even novice teachers are prepared for power struggles with students and are able to deal with them effectively. They tend to be less prepared, though, for the political climate which might have the potential to set up power struggles with other teachers and subordinates such as well-established teachers' aides. How can these situations be avoided? If these situations appear unavoidable, how can they be modified in order to preempt behavior management problems from students who understand that their teacher is not the person in charge?

    4.2   <u>Collaboration</u>: Collaboration with teachers' aides, other special educators, and regular teacher are essential if special education students' needs are to be met. In many instances, for example, behavior plans are constructed among all these professionals so that there will be consistent implementation of behavioral interventions across different settings and with different teachers. What potential problems can arise in student behavioral intervention when the social climate among the staff is so tense? How can teachers communicate a different, more appropriate climate to students?

4.3   Student Compliance: The case shows that Pat is able to impose a certain type of behavior management effectively. The aide is able to control the class and make them more compliant. What are the ramifications for student behavior when they perceive the teachers' aide as having more authority than the teacher? How can teachers confront other professionals who overstep their bounds of authority to the detriment of the students and professional conduct? How can teachers remedy such a situation without causing further damage to professional relationships? How can teachers modify the requirements of behavior management to more suit their style of teaching and to emulate less the style of a predecessor?

4.4   Professional Support: Teachers like Jeannette find themselves with very little professional support as they try to deal with these dilemmas. How can the garner more support for their professional perceptions and to get better cooperation for improved behavior management?

WINNIE: Patty Gray

1.   Case Summary

Characters: Narrator (Patty Gray), First Grade Teacher.
Jackie, Consulting Teacher.
Winnie, First Grade Student.
Mr. B, Principal.
Betsy, Kindergarten Teacher.

Winnie (Winslow) is the only first-grade student in the class who has not been retained from the previous year. The narrator writing to her journal (Patty Gray) is looking forward to her second year of teaching although she has not dealt with at-risk students previously. Betsy, Winnie's kindergarten teacher, informs Patty of Winnie's problems the previous year. Among Winnie's characteristic attention-seeking and oppositional behaviors is his habit of following the teacher around the class, including to the bathroom. Winnie's social perceptions and attention-seeking behaviors are inappropriate, and for the duration of the case he does not appear to improve much, in spite of a number of interventions that Patty thinks up, solutions from Jackie (the consulting teacher), and persistence in maintaining all the behavioral interventions.

At the end of the case, Patty is left frustrated by her inability to effectively change Winnie's behavior, but she feels a sense of accomplishment in that Winnie's reading skills improved significantly over the year.

2.   Special Features

Patty has little experience in teaching at-risk students, but she feels confident that the year ahead will be a worthwhile challenge. Winnie's reputation precedes him, and Patty soon discovers that Winnie's distractibility, explosive behavior, continual attention-seeking and immature social skills. Patty appropriately seeks assistance from the consulting teacher, but initial interventions and those subsequently modified proved relatively ineffective. However, Winnie does make progress with his reading. Patty persistently applied several more behavioral interventions which, by the end of the case, have failed to effectively address Winnie's maladjustment.

3.   Teaching Strategy

Teachers sometimes encounter student with behavior problems that prove resistant to change in spite of persistent application of behavioral procedures. In many cases the behavioral change is absent due to misapplication of interventions, or the utilizations of inappropriate interventions. There are times, however, when appropriate interventions prove of little help. Teachers sometimes deal with students whose behavior holds little promise of improving, although such a judgement can only be made after all possible intervention alternatives have been exhausted.

4.   Blocks of Analysis

   4.1   Class Composition: The class consists mostly of children who are "at-risk" and who have already been identified as having school problems. Winnie, however, is not a repeating student. What is the potential for Winnie to succeed in this setting? Why are students like Winnie placed in class like this?

4.2   Gender of Students: There are more boys than girls in the class, a common occurrence among students with behavior problems. Why are boys overrepresented in classes where students with behavior problems are found? What are the problems that might arise in terms of behavior management in a class composed of many more boys than girls?

4.3   Medication to Control Behavior: Some of the students are receiving Ritalin, apparently because they are "active." What are the ethical issues surrounding the use of medication for "active students?" Are there instances when medication should or should not be administered?

4.4   Immature Behavior: Winnie shows many signs of immature and inappropriate behavior throughout the case. Are these behaviors generally amenable to change? What is preventing the modification of Winnie's behavior in the classroom? How do teachers judge whether inappropriate behaviors are immature or indicators of potential serious problems?

4.5   Attention-seeking Behavior: Winnie demonstrates a particularly inappropriate form of attention-seeking (following the teacher to the bathroom). This behavior is both inappropriate and indicative of the need for social skill training. How can teachers reduce instances of this kind of behavior without making the student feel rejected?

4.6   Consulting Activity: The teacher consults Jackie for assistance in dealing with Winnie. What possible problems could arise from this arrangement? How do teachers know when they need help or whether they are simply not doing enough to take care of their class? What options remain when the recommendations of the consulting teacher fail to resolve the behavior management issues?

4.7   Escalation of Inappropriate Behavior After Behavioral Intervention: Intervention by the teacher does not result in more appropriate behavior, but rather Winnie appears to become more bothersome. Are there ways of avoiding such an escalation? How do teachers decide when continued escalation of inappropriate behavior is a result of the intervention or whether a longer time is needed before modifying the intervention?

4.8   Modification of Behavioral Intervention: Jackie and Patty correctly decide to modify the behavioral intervention when previous interventions prove ineffective. What are the criteria for changing behavioral interventions? How do teachers evaluate whether a new intervention will be effective or not? How do teachers asses whether a new intervention may be even more detrimental than the intervention presently in place?

4.9   Change of Inappropriate Behavior: The case makes clear that after extensive intervention, Winnie's immature behavior changes to a different configuration. How can teachers anticipate such changes? How should new inappropriate behaviors be evaluated in relation to existing consequences for inappropriate behaviors?

107

4.10   Student Fear of Failure: Winnie overreacts when he finds out that he has missed some words on a spelling test. His behavior indicates that he may be afraid of failure, and that--at least in part--his inappropriate behavior stems from a fear of failure. How can teachers teach students that part of learning is making mistakes? How do teachers asses the extent to which inappropriate behavior can be attributed to fear of failure?

4.11   Positive Peer Reinforcement: The teacher uses the rest of the class to reinforce Winnie's appropriate behavior. What are the ethical issues surrounding the use of peers to reinforce appropriate behavior of other students? How do teachers modify peer reinforcement of inappropriate behavior?

4.12   Reasoning With students About Their Behavior: The teacher attempts to reason with Winnie about his inappropriate behavior in the hope that the appeal to reason will prevent further misbehavior. What are the advantages and disadvantages of appealing to students' reason when they misbehave?

YOU HAD BETTER GET ON THEM: Bob Winters

1. Case Summary

    Characters: Bob Winters, Middle School Teacher.
                  Mr. Dudley, Principal.
                  Lawrence, Cathy, Ronnie, Gerald, Mike, Linwood, Students.

    Bob begins his new job teaching students he has not been trained to teach. Mr. Dudley makes it clear that Bob will be responsible for major teaching decisions and that the school generally expects tight control of the students' behavior. Bob finds the students more academically able than he expected and his teaching solutions, geared by his training to preschool students, leaves the students bored and prone to disruption and inappropriate behavior. Bob copes in the best way he can, but he is unable to adjust his teaching to the academic level of the class.

    Slowly the situation becomes unmanageable. The students become increasingly less motivated, they ignore Bob's directives, and horseplay becomes more common. The misbehavior escalates to the point that noise from Bob's classroom spills into the hallway. Mr. Dudley appears in the classroom doorway and, in front of Bob, firmly admonishes the class, who are quick to comply. The episode leaves Bob feeling ineffective, embarrassed and powerless.

    Bob resolves to "toughen up." He tries several punitive measures which seem to work for a few days, but generally his ineffectiveness increases and his solutions become more punishing. The cycle of misbehavior and punishment escalates until Bob, exasperated, tells a student to "Get your ass in the chair" and sends Cathy to the office for nudging Linwood in response to this harsh statement.

    Cathy returns to the classroom accompanied by Mr. Dudley, who asks to see Bob in the hallway. As Cathy returns to her seat, she announces to the class that she has told Mr. Dudley what Bob said to the class.

2. Special Features

    Bob begins the year at a disadvantage because he is teaching students that he has not been trained to teach and he fails to adjust according to the learning needs of the class. Furthermore, he is baffled by the students' escalation of inappropriate behavior. He realizes that he is losing control and resorts to punitive interventions which only add fuel to the fire.

    Bob is also losing on another front: Mr. Dudley is aware of the problems and enhances Bob's ineffectiveness by intervening to get the class quiet. The class knows that Bob does not command their respect or compliance and realize that they can use Mr. Dudley against Bob. When Bob finally loses his temper, Cathy is quick to tell Mr. Dudley what Bob said.

3. Teaching Strategy

    Many novice teachers find it difficult to adjust to their classes at the beginning of the school year, especially if it is their first teaching assignment. These difficulties are compounded by teaching students out of one's area of expertise. Behavior management requires a great deal of forethought and a constant "fine tuning" to gain the respect and compliance of the students for learning. It takes a great amount of skill to realize when one intervention is ineffective and when it is time to change to another. Reading behavioral clues of when to change interventions requires a deep awareness of why students are behaving the way they are.

On the other hand, many teachers are acutely aware that they are being ineffective and fail to ask for assistance, believing that they will blindly hit on the "correct" solution to the behavior management problem. Usually this leads to chaotic experiences like the one faced by Bob in this case.

4.   Blocks of Analysis

4.1   Teaching out of Field: It is relatively common for special educators to teach outside of their field of expertise. Such situations can present very real problems in meeting the learning needs of the students. Teaching out of field also has important ramifications for behavior management. For example, there are many different behavior management techniques appropriate for preschoolers that are inappropriate in dealing with high school students. What classroom conditions will help teachers in this position to adjust and effectively manage the behavior of their students? How can teachers adjust more effectively? How do teachers decide when one behavior management approach must be abandoned in favor of another?

4.2   Expectations for Behavior Management: Many teachers, shortly after beginning their job, become aware that they are expected to deal with their students in a certain way. The expectations of the local school community, the principal, and of more experienced teachers may or may not correspond with the new teacher's outlook for behavior management. How do teachers reconcile their behavior management styles to fit the expectations of the school community? Should they try to adjust or attempt to "go it alone?" What are the practical consequences of these options in terms of how student classroom behavior will be influenced?

4.3   Collaboration: Many special education students are mainstreamed into regular classes. The behavior management techniques employed in the special education class may be mediated by the management techniques used by regular education teachers. What are the best ways of ensuring that behavior management is consistent across settings? How can collaboration with regular educators best be achieved?

4.4   Classroom Setting: The case makes it clear that one major factor that leads to inappropriate behavior is the way Bob structures learning time. There are strong connections between the classroom structure for learning and student behavior. What are the best ways to ensure that the classroom setting for learning supports a teacher's behavior management approaches? How can the classroom setting be modified to ensure that students not only learn, but that they behave in an appropriate way?

4.5   Motivation: The students in this case are not motivated. This is partially a result of their mild disabilities, but also part of a reaction to the structure of the class. How can teachers use behavior management as a means of motivating students? What classroom settings and behavior management techniques are conducive to increasing motivation for learning and appropriate behavior?

4.6   Intervention of Other Staff: Many teachers having problems with behavior management find themselves in the embarrassing position of having other members of the school staff intervene on their behalf. Are such interventions always inappropriate? What are the potential consequences of such interventions? How can a teacher prevent such interventions from happening?

4.7   Differential Structure Levels: Bob learns that the more structure he imposes on his low SES students, the better they respond. Is this an appropriate behavior management perception? Should students from different socio-economic levels be managed in different ways?

4.8   Control issues: Often, teachers of students with mild handicaps find themselves in serious power struggles for control of the class. If teachers engage in these battles, they often alienate themselves from their students and become ineffective educators. How can teachers avoid such struggles? If a teacher loses the power struggle, how can he or she regain authority and control for learning?

4.9   Burn-Out: Teachers often become frustrated because their behavior management solutions do not work. They become frustrated and begin to implement harsher (and usually more punitive, and less effective) behavior management plans. Often, these measures, rather than helping, escalate the inappropriate behavior of the students. What steps can teachers take to reverse this trend?

4.10   Generic Behavior Management Solutions: Teachers sometimes use a generic "one fits all" approach to behavior management. They assume that a single technique is equally effective for all students. When are "generic" solutions appropriate? How can teachers judge the effectiveness of these kinds of solutions? What are the consequences of having different behavioral interventions for some students and not for others?

4.11   Trial and Error learning: Teachers sometimes move randomly from one failed behavioral intervention to another. How should teachers decide whether an alternative management approach is appropriate? How can they project its effectiveness? What other ways can teachers use to better decide the potential effectiveness of alternative behavior interventions?

References

Bell, R. Q., & Harper, L. V. (1977). Child effects on adults. Hillsdale NJ: Lawrence Erlbaum Associates.

Brown, J. S., Collins, A., & Duguid, P. (1989). Situated cognition and the culture of learning. Educational Researcher, 18(1), 32-42.

Carter, K., & Unklesbay, R. (1989). Cases in teaching and law. Journal of Curriculum Studies, 21(6), 527-536.

Christensen, C. R. (1987). Teaching and the case method. Boston MA: Harvard Business School.

Clark, C., & Lampert, M. (1986). The study of teacher thinking: Implications for teacher education. Journal of Teacher Education, 37(5), 27-31.

Collins, A., Brown, J. S., Newman, S. E. (1989). In L. B. Resnick (Ed.), Knowing, learning, and instruction: Essays in honor of Robert Glaser. Hillsdale NJ: Lawrence Erlbaum Associates.

Feiman-Nemser, S. (1990). Teacher preparation: Structural and conceptual alternatives. In W. R. Houston (Ed.), Handbook of research on teacher education. New York: MacMillan.

Gage, N. L., & Needels, M. C., Process-product research on teaching: A review of criticisms. The Elementary School Journal, 89(3), 253-299.

Kennedy, M. (1987). Inexact sciences: Professional education and the development of expertise. In E. Rothkopf (Ed.), Review of research in education (pp. 133-167). Washington DC: American Educational Research Association.

Kleinfeld, J. (1988). Learning to think like a teacher: The study of cases. Fairbanks AL: University of Alaska, Center for Cross-Cultural Studies.

Kleinfeld, J. (1991, April). Changes in problem solving abilities of students taught through case methods. Paper presented at the American Educational Research Association, Chicago IL.

Kounin, J. (1970). Discipline and group management in classrooms. New York: Holt, Rinehardt, & Winston.

Larrivee, B. (1985). Effective teaching for successful mainstreaming. New York: Longman.

Lave, J. (1988). Cognition in practice: Mind, mathematics, and culture in everyday life. Boston MA: Cambridge University Press.

Lave, J., & Wenger, E. (in preparation). Situated learning: Legitimate peripheral participation.

Merseth, K. K. (1991). The case for cases in teacher education. Washington DC: American Association for Higher Education and American Association of Colleges for Teacher Education.

112

Morine-Dershimer, G. (1991, June). <u>Case methods in teacher education: Where do they fit?</u> Paper presented at The Case Method in Teacher Education: A Working Conference, James Madison University, Harrisonburg VA.

Rogoff, B. (1984). Introduction: Thinking and learning in social context. In B. Rogoff & J. Lave (Eds.), <u>Everyday cognition: Its development in social context</u> (pp. 1-8). Cambridge MA: Harvard University Press.

Rosenshine, B. (1983). Teaching functions in instructional programs. <u>The Elementary School Journal, 83</u>(4), 335-354.

Rowe, M. B. (1974). Relation of wait-time and reward to the development of language, logic, and fate control: Part II--Rewards. <u>Journal of Research in Science Teaching, 11</u>(4), 291-308.

Shulman, L. S. (1986). Those who understand: Knowledge and growth in teaching. <u>Educational Researcher, 15</u>(2), 4-14.

Silverman, R., Welty, W. M., & Lyon, S. (1992). <u>Case studies for teacher problem solving</u>. New York: McGraw-Hill.

Spiro, R. J., Vispoel, W. P., Schmitz, J., Samarapungavan, A., & Boerger, A. E. (1987). Knowledge acquisition for application: Cognitive flexibility and transfer in complex context domains. In B. Britton (Ed.), <u>Executive control processes</u> (pp. 177-199). Hillsdale NJ: Lawrence Erlbaum Associates.

White, B. C., & McNergney, R. F. (1991, June). <u>Case-based teacher education: The state of the art.</u>

White, J. B. (1985). <u>Heracles' bow: Essays on the rhetoric and poetics of the law.</u> Madison WI: University of Wisconsin Press.

Zeichner, K. M., & Liston, D. P. (1990). Traditions of reform in U. S. teacher education. <u>Journal of Teacher Education, 41</u>(2), 3-20.

NOTES

NOTES

NOTES